THE ASIAN HOUSE

The Asian House

CONTEMPORARY HOUSES OF SOUTHEAST ASIA

Robert Powell

PERIPLUS

This edition published in 1999 by
Periplus Editions (HK) Ltd

Original edition published by
Select Books Pte Ltd, Singapore
Copyright © 1999, 1995, 1993
Select Books Pte Ltd

Designed by
Duet Design Pte Ltd

Typecasting by Superskill Graphics Pte Ltd
Colour separation by Colourscan Co Pte Ltd
Printed by SNP Printing Pte Ltd

ISBN : 962-593-329-8

ACKNOWLEDGEMENTS

Many individuals have assisted me in identifying the houses illustrated in this book. I am grateful for the help of Pisit Rojanavanich (Thailand), Tan Hock Beng (Singapore), Eko Budihardjo (Indonesia), Mathar Bunnag (Thailand), Sumet Jumsai (Thailand) and Adhi Moersid (Indonesia). No one helped me more in this respect than Emmanuel Miñana (Philippines).

I appreciate the time that numerous architects have taken to talk to me about issues that concern them and the current state of architecture in the region. I have been greatly assisted by the critical insights of Tay Kheng Soon and William Lim in Singapore, also Jimmy Lim and Dr Ken Yeang in Malaysia. The comments of my colleagues at the National University of Singapore, particularly Dr PG Raman, have been valuable and I have been well supported by Ho Pak Toe, Director of the School of Architecture.

I am indebted to Suha Özkan, Secretary General of the Aga Khan Award for Architecture in Geneva, for inviting me to attend several Award seminars. A paper delivered at an AKAA seminar in Zanzibar by Hasan-Uddin Khan and Charles Moore provided the inspiration for this book.

For their hospitality I thank particularly Tengku Zainal Adlin in Sabah, Prof Parmono Atmadi in Yogyakarta, Drs Sunaryo in Bandung, Gordon and Tricia Benton in Jakarta, Solichin and Ani Gunawan in Jakarta, Ado Escudero, Bobby and Denise Mañosa, Leandro 'Lindy' Locsin, Patis Tesoro, and Ruby Diaz Roa in Manila.

I am also indebted to Associate Professor Pussadee Tiptus and Associate Professor Prapapat Niyom of Chulalongkorn University in Thailand, Nithi Sthapitanonda (Thailand), Theeraphon Niyom (Thailand), Dr Ismeth Abidin (Indonesia), Budji Layug (Philippines), Kevin Tan Ming Yew (Singapore), Robi Sularto (Indonesia), and Tang Guan Bee (Singapore).

Dra Erna Nur Eddin and Dra Adreati R Kusuma of Laras Magazine in Indonesia were welcoming and assisted me in identifying houses in Java and Bali.

Dato Paduka Ibrahim Hj Mohammed (Brunei), Indra RD Abidin (Jakarta), Wong Kah Ho (Sabah), Prabhakorn Vadanuakul (Bangkok), Hendra Hadiprana (Jakarta), Suchart Subhasavasdikul (Bangkok), and Rodolfo Giusti de Marle (Bali) were gracious and hospitable on my travels.

There are undoubtedly many exemplary houses in Southeast Asia which should have been included but which I am not aware of. There are also a number of houses which cannot be published because of their owners' desire for privacy. I am therefore doubly grateful to those owners who have allowed me to intrude into their homes and I hope they will not be offended when I offer my architectural criticism and commentary.

I have been fortunate, as with all my previous books, to be assisted by Lynda Lim who has, with infinite patience, processed the numerous drafts of the manuscript. Lena Lim U Wen, the publisher, has given consistent support to the project, for which I am indebted and I trust she will find her faith justified. Thanks are also due to editor, Chu Chu Yuan for her comments on and corrections to the text.

The design of the book is by Ko Hui-Huy and David McElwaine of Duet Design. The plans and sections have been beautifully and sensitively redrawn by Neo Sei Hwa, Un Wai Kay and Quek Ser Bock, from original drawings supplied by the architects.

Finally to Shantheni, who has been constantly supportive, my thanks and my love.

- Robert Powell
Singapore 1992

CONTENTS

Contemporary Houses of Southeast Asia   10
Robert Powell

I. USING VERNACULAR FORMS AND MATERIALS   18

The Tesoro Rest House   Laguna, Philippines   20
Designers: Conrado A Escudero and Patis Tesoro

The Giusti House   Sanur, Bali, Indonesia   24
Designer: Rodolfo Giusti de Marle

The Sunaryo House   Bandung, Java, Indonesia   30
Designer: Sunaryo

The Moersid House   Jakarta, Java, Indonesia   36
Architect: Adhi Moersid . Atelier Enam

The Mañosa House   Alabang, Manila, Philippines   40
Architect: Francisco 'Bobby' Mañosa

II. TRANSFORMING THE VERNACULAR   46

The Roa House   Alabang, Manila, Philippines   48
Architects: GF and Partners

The Eu House   Damansara, Kuala Lumpur, Malaysia   54
Architect: Jimmy Lim . CSL Associates

The Precima House   Bangsar, Kuala Lumpur, Malaysia 60
Architect: Jimmy Lim . CSL Associates

The Wong House   Singapore   66
Architects: William Lim Associates

The Indra Abidin House   Jakarta, Java, Indonesia   72
Architect: Ismeth Abidin

The Tiptus House   Bangkok, Thailand   76
Architects: Boonyawat and Pussadee Tiptus

The Bin Tong Park House   Singapore   82
Architect: Ernesto Bedmar . Bedmar and Shi

The Locsin House   Makati, Metro Manila, Philippines 90
Architect: Leandro V Locsin

III. INCORPORATING COLONIAL INFLUENCES *74*

The Reuter House Singapore *96*
Architects: William Lim Associates

The Gunawan House Jakarta, Java, Indonesia *104*
Architects: Tan Tjiang Ay, Solichin Gunawan and Ani Isdiati

IV. REINTERPRETING THE EXTENDED FAMILY COMPOUND *108*

Bann Ton Son Bangkok, Thailand *126*
Architects: Prapapat and Theeraphon Niyom . Plan Architects

The Hadiprana House Tanah Gajah, Bali, Indonesia *116*
Architects: Hendra Hadiprana and Faried Masdoeki . Grahacipta Hadiprana

V. FUSING MODERNITY WITH THE VERNACULAR *124*

Bann Soi Klang Bangkok, Thailand *126*
Architect: Nithi Sthapitanonda . Architects 49

Bann Rim Nam Bangkok, Thailand *132*
Architect: Nithi Sthapitanonda . Architects 49

The Lo House Kota Kinabalu, Sabah, Malaysia *136*
Architect: Wong Kah Ho . WaY Architects

The Razak Harris House Kota Kinabalu, Sabah, Malaysia *140*
Architect: Wong Kah Ho . WaY Architects

The Vacharphol House Bangkok, Thailand *146*
Architect: John Rifenberg . Rifenberg Associates

The Tengku Adlin House Kota Kinabalu, Sabah, Malaysia *152*
Architect: Lee Seng Loong . Leesengloong Architects

The Zulueta House Tagatay City, Philippines *156*
Designer: Budji Layug

The Roof Roof House Selangor, Malaysia *162*
Architects: Kenneth Yeang . TR Hamzah and Yeang

The Mountbatten Road House Singapore *166*
Architect: Tang Guan Bee . Tangguanbee Architects

Selected Bibliography . Glossary . Photography Credits *172*

"For most people in traditional societies, the house has been an extension of the human body, an outer layer of clothing, not unlike that of other people's but capable of accommodating an extra amount of effort, of care, of ornament and of self-expression that lets its occupants inhabit it.

The houses of the rich have always been the major indicators of architectural change. Through them the aspirations and the reflections of self-image are made most apparent. They act as models for others in a filtering down effect."

- Hasan-Uddin Khan

During a momentus week in September 1991, whilst I was researching houses in the Philippines, the senate debated the issue of the continued USA presence at the Subic Naval Base. On Monday 9th September by a narrow margin, the senators voted to end the lease on the base. At the heart of the matter was the question of Philippine 'independence' of American influence – symbolically the base represented for many Filipinos a colonial presence.

Three decades earlier Malaysia, Singapore and Indonesia went through a struggle for their independence from the British and Dutch administrations. The process was painful and sometimes bloody, and has left a legacy – a complicated relationship with Europe and America.

On the one hand, the countries of Southeast Asia welcome the benefits of modernisation and international trade but, on the other hand, there is a desire by many to retain or reestablish their local roots, and to resist Western hegemony and the homogenisation of world cultures.

This situation has been expressed in terms of an identity crisis which has its implications in architectural expressions. It has also been expressed in terms of 'Regionalism' in architecture.[1] Regionalism is not simply the nostalgic privileging of the vernacular form but a synthesis of the vernacular with modernism. It is a way of thinking about architecture which is culturally regenerative – not a style, but a search for cultural continuity in the aftermath of the colonial experience. It implies the embracing of modernism whilst simultaneously maintaining links with traditional forms and practices.

A Spectrum of Ideas

The private houses in this book represent a spectrum of responses to cultural changes in Southeast Asia. All but two have been designed and built in the last ten years, a period of rapid change and economic growth in the region.

To understand each house; its form, hierarchy and spatial arrangement, it is necessary to 'excavate' through several layers of cultural influences.

In the contemporary houses of Southeast Asia, the influence of the vernacular, that is to say, the houses built by the native inhabitants, can be readily identified. Superimposed upon this are the influences of immigrants chiefly from China and the Indian sub-continent. Overlaid upon this are layers of colonial influence; principally that of the British in Malaysia, Brunei and Singapore, the Dutch in Indonesia, and those of the Spanish and Americans in the Philippines. These are bonded with layers of religious influences from Christianity, Buddhism, Hinduism, and Islam. Overarching all of these are the forces of rapid urbanisation and modernisation of contemporary society.

The choice of chapter headings reflects this multifaceted process. There is a degree of ambiguity in the titles which reflects a reluctance to attach labels, but some categorisation was deemed necessary to give clarity to the text.

The houses are a barometer of taste and of changing attitudes. They meet modern requirements yet, in a variety of expressions, they embrace traditional forms, customs and materials.

Many have traditional spatial arrangements, combined with, overlaid by, or in synthesis with imported Western-inspired ideas. Others draw on forms deeply embedded in the collective memories of the diverse peoples of Southeast Asia. Cosmological models surface again and again. The result is a 'hybrid' architecture. This book is arranged to represent the spectrum of approaches. No attempt is made to privilege any of the diverse expressions, neither the reuse of vernacular forms and materials at one end of the spectrum, or the modernist-inspired response at the other.

The houses, with some exceptions, are owned by royal princes, directors of multi-national corporations, successful business people, accountants and architects. The owners may be collectively termed the well-educated and relatively wealthy. It is often those who can afford to build their own houses and to commission architects to design them who determine the aspirations of others.

This is not to suggest that success in public or commercial life is synonymous with good taste, indeed there are many examples to the contrary, but in the best scenario a person building a dwelling for his or her family reflects upon the significance of privacy, the display of wealth, symbolism, the family's lifestyle, social conventions and perhaps *feng-shui*. (Taylor 1987)

The architect-designed house may be considered by some to be superfluous in the context of the massive housing shortages in the Philippines, Malaysia, Thailand and Indonesia, particularly in the urban area. Less than 1% of the population in any country can afford the services of an architect; yet individual houses provide the exemplars which mass-produced housing attempts to emulate. (Serageldin 1990)

In the different context of modernism, houses such as Falling Water by Frank Lloyd Wright and Villa Savoye by Le Corbusier moulded the ideas of a whole generation, not only in America and Europe, but throughout the world via the hundreds of architectural students who studied these designs. "They became a symbol of their age reflecting values and aspirations."[2] (Fig.1)

These houses became models to be emulated. In a similar manner the houses illustrated in this book will hopefully, help to fashion the consciousness of young architects and prospective house builders in Asia and beyond.

Fig. 1 Houses such as Falling Water by Frank Lloyd Wright (the Kaufmann House, Pennsylvania, USA, 1935) moulded the ideas of a generation throughout the world.

The Models for Contemporary Houses

The models for the individual houses in this book stem from what Hasan-Uddin Khan has referred to as "two separate strands of culture: the 'modern' (international) and the 'traditional' (vernacular). The former is Western or Japanese and incorporates advanced technology, the latter interprets the local vernacular".[3] These come together in a multitude of architectural expressions.

Thus contemporary houses in Southeast Asia range from those which are close to the vernacular in terms of form, materials, method of construction and low-energy technology; to others which clearly demonstrate, in their white planar surfaces or fragmented form, the influence of modernist and deconstructivist ideas, which add an international dimension.

The Traditional Strand

The vernacular house in Southeast Asia is often a reflection of social position and of cultural patterns, and where these same patterns are expressed in contemporary houses they result in specific spatial arrangements. (Taylor 1987. Fig.2)

"In most houses of the Orient clear distinctions are evident between reception areas for strangers or acquaintances and areas for family activities."[4] There are hierarchies of spaces for public display of wealth, for semi-private reception and for intimate private use. (Fig.3)

A number of the houses illustrated have this clear spatial hierarchy and subconsciously one is aware of thresholds between these spaces.

Climate and lifestyles in tropical Asia make the open terrace or pavilion a constant theme. Again, this is drawn from the vernacular; the Malay *kampong* house, or the Filipino *nipa* hut. It takes the form in the tropics of an open-sided verandah, a *lanai*, a *serambi*, a *pendopo* or a sleeping deck.

Fig. 2 The vernacular house in Southeast Asia is often a reflection of social position. The chief's house at Bawomataluo, South Nias, off the west coast of Sumatra (after Shroder, 1917).

Fig. 3 In most traditional houses there are hierarchies of spaces for public display, semi-private reception and intimate privacy. A Malay house in Kampong Duyung, Malacca display these distinctions (after Lim Jee Yuan, 1987).

Trihatakarama/Tri Angga

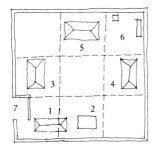

utaming nista	utaming madya	utama
madyaning nista	madyaning madya	madya
nistaning nista	nistaning madya	nista

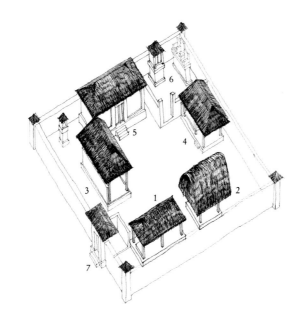

1 kitchen (*paon*)
2 granary (*jineng lumbung*)
3 guest bedroom
4 adults bedroom and for
 boys of the family
5 head of the house
 (*uta mete*) also bedroom
 for unmarried girls
6 family temple (*pamerajan*)
7 gate

Fig. 4 Cosmological models frequently determine the spatial organisation of houses. A nine-square *mandala* theoretically underlies this traditional house form in Southern Bali (after Dumarçay, 1987).

Traditional houses were not simply shelter from the tropical climate but, they also, according to Waterson, "involve the creation of social and symbolic space – which both mirrors and moulds the world view of its creators and inhabitants". The house in Southeast Asia has traditionally been a microcosm of the cosmos, "reflecting in its layout, structure and ornamentation, a concept of an ideal natural and social order".[5] These models of the cosmos surface again and again; for example, in the nine square *mandala* which underlies the spatial organisation of several of the house plans. (Fig.4)

Our fascination with vernacular built forms is intuitive and is, says Papanek, "a recognition of forms and patterns that speak a nearly universal language that is deeply rooted in our collective unconscious memory".[6]

In the past people lived in dwellings that were constructed of materials found locally and which were a purely instinctive response to the tropical climate and the ecology (Fig.5). At the 'vernacular' end of the spectrum of contemporary Asian houses, the same instinctive, sensitive responses are evidently flourishing. Several houses are embedded in their context, in a symbiotic relationship with nature.

An understanding of the vernacular built form is increasingly relevant to designing contemporary houses. Quoting Frank Lloyd Wright, Papanek notes: "The true basis for the serious study of the art of architecture lies with indigenous humble buildings everywhere. They are to architecture what folklore is to literature, or folksong to music... Functions are truthfully conceived and rendered invariably with natural feeling. Results are often beautiful and always instructive."[7]

Fig. 5 In the past people lived in dwellings that were built with materials found locally and which were an instinctive response to climate. The *Bahay Kubo*, a *nipa* hut found in the Philippines (after Klassen, 1986).

Fig. 6 Traditional central plains, cluster house in Thailand which is the precedence for the two houses in Bangkok (after Warren, 1988).

Fig. 7 The colonial influence is part of the collective memory of most Southeast Asian countries. Black and white house, Nassim Road, typical of many built in Singapore from 1910 to 1930 (after Lee Kip Lin, 1988).

Thus it is to the humble *nipa* hut that several architects in the Philippines turn in their search for an appropriate form for a contemporary dwelling. It is the traditional house on stilts alongside the Chao Phrya River in Thailand that is the precedence for the homes of two families in Bangkok. (Fig.6)

The colonial influence is also part of the collective memory of most Southeast Asian countries and these memories surface in two houses; one in Jakarta and the other in Singapore. (Fig.7)

When architects design by using traditional houses as exemplars, it is necessary, however, to be critical. The design of the individual house, "should be a subtle recollection of a culture. It should be a distillation process. It is necessary to look for an internal structure, or an internal hierarchy in the traditional house and to look at what it is as a symbol".[8]

The International Strand

Often the international dimension in a contemporary Asian house is the result of the house owner or the architect having received their education in America or Europe. Also the Western media penetrates all aspects of life in Southeast Asia; European and American (and increasingly Japanese) architectural publications showing house models are pervasive. The resultant exposure to Western intellectual traditions and architectural trends is manifested in the reproduction of spatial arrangements, materials and architectural languages more familiar in Western cultures.

The international strand of culture is expressed through the architectural ideas of the Modern Movement, Post-Modernism and Deconstruction.

The Modern Movement was concerned with abstraction and the "reality of modern life"[9] – a secular mass culture which excluded ornament, metaphor, symbolism and historical reference. These ideas are expressed in the architecture of Le Corbusier and Mies van der Rohe. (Fig.8)

Some houses in this book are clearly inspired by the Modernist ideology and they represent the other end of the spectrum of approaches. (Fig.9)

The Role of Individual Houses as Exemplars

The owners of the houses in this book whether indigenous to the region or expatriates simultaneously have an international outlook and a local perspective and their interests often reflect a deep awareness of ecology and history. This is evidenced in the care that they have lavished upon the design of their homes and the interiors. The houses would not have taken their specific form had the owners not thought deeply about their own cultural values.[10]

The choice of materials, the openness of the plan or otherwise, the extent of high technology incorporated into the design and the relationship between members of the family all reflect the owner's and the architect's stance in relation to the notions of modernism and tradition.

The relation of the family to society is also expressed through the house form and the owner's attitude to ecological matters and to cultural continuity is revealed. Houses thus, "operate as signifiers in society to denote relative social position, lifestyle, conformity or non-conformity, the taste and preferences of the occupants".[11]

Furthermore the houses of the wealthy, "become part of the domain of signs on which all architects draw today. The presence of such exemplars is what defines both the aspirations of people and the consciousnesss of architects. Ultimately it is what helps fashion reality".[12]

Fig. 8 The Modern Movement excluded ornament and historical reference. Le Corbusier, Villa Savoye, Poissy, 1928-30.

Populist Architecture

The development of industrial societies that has resulted in separating the construction of houses into different fields of activity: architect, builder, owner and end-user has had many negative consequences.

Also, with the increasingly rapid rate of urbanisation in Southeast Asia, societies such as that of Singapore's have moved from predominantly *kampong* life to city life in less than three generations. There are attendant problems and an absence of good models for contemporary houses. There is much bad taste in evidence and societies in rapid transition indiscriminately borrow models from other cultures.

Condemning this bad taste in Singapore's domestic architecture, architect Tay Kheng Soon has used the phrase '*obiang* architecture'[13], a term which could be equally applied to the architecture of other countries in Southeast Asia.

There is evidence in the houses of the dominant elite in Kuala Lumpur, Kota Kinabalu, Jakarta, Bangkok and Bandar Seri Begawan of the uncritical use of Post-Modern Classicism often badly interpreted in terms of proportion, form and scale. Overweighted broken pediments, badly proportioned columns, and other incongruous architectural features abound often in an eclectic combination, whilst the indigenous vernacular architecture is often rejected as backward and incompatible with a modernising society.

One might ask, what does the use of the Post-Modern Classical architectural language tell us about the owners and the architects? It seems distinctly odd to take as an expression of emerging architectural identity, a style which is more commonly associated with political domination and colonial power.

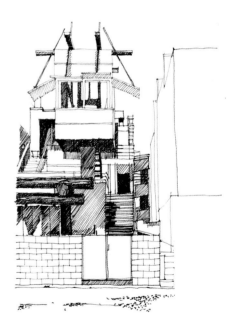

Fig. 9 The work of so-called Deconstructivists such as Frank Gehry is part of the international strand of influences. The Norton House, Venice Beach, LA, 1983.

It poses the question of who is really concerned with cultural continuity. Is it something that society as a whole turns to when it has achieved the material benefits of life and, so to speak, enters the 'self-actualisation' stage that Maslow defines in terms of individual development? Is it inevitable that Southeast Asian cultures will go through a period of destruction of their heritage in the process of urban renewal and economic growth, before belatedly appreciating the houses designed by architects like Jimmy Lim in Malaysia, Bobby Mañosa in the Philippines, Boonyawat and Pussadee Tiptus in Thailand and William Lim Associates in Singapore?

The Architect/Client Relationship

For the architect the design of a house for an individual is one of the most rewarding yet demanding tasks. Rarely will the designer have such a close working relationship with the end user; more often the 'client' is a committee or a government authority and the eventual occupant of the architect's creativity somewhat remote. This is true when an architect is employed upon the design of mass housing.

The most successful houses arise out of a close empathy between client and designer. This relationship is essential and it would not seem to matter which is the dominant partner.

When selecting an architect for the design of a dwelling, this matter of empathy is of critical importance; for the relationship can never be based totally on professional qualifications. It inevitably becomes a meeting of attitudes and temperaments. The house becomes a portrait of the owner.

Several of the houses in this book are designed by architects for their own use. Here the houses are uncompromising expressions of the architects' own values and attitudes towards cultural continuity and the synthesis of modernism and tradition.

In the following pages the many facets of the synthesis are revealed. Readers will doubtless place themselves at some point in the spectrum of ideas, according to their own attitude towards cultural continuity and change.

"Private houses are social portraits of their clients."

- David Cohn, 1990

---

[1] An Aga Khan Award for Architecture (AKAA) seminar in Kuala Lumpur (1984) discussed the question of an identity 'crisis' in architecture. This was published as *Architecture and Identity*, AKAA/ Concept Media, Singapore, 1986. Two years later the question of Regionalism was discussed at a seminar in Bangladesh. This was published as *Regionalism in Architecture*, AKAA/Concept Media, Singapore, 1987.

[2] Ismail Serageldin remarks on this in the book *The Architecture of Housing*, Aga Khan Award for Architecture, Geneva, Nov 1990. Houses such as Falling Water and Villa Savoye, he contends, become part of the domain of signs from which architects draw inspiration.

[3] Khan, Hasan-Uddin referred to these two aspects in a paper presented at a seminar in Zanzibar in Oct 1988. It is recorded in *The Architecture of Housing*, Aga Khan Award for Architecture, Geneva, Nov 1990, pp.165-187.

Khan's idea of a 'spectrum' of approaches provided the basis for this book. His paper was subsequently published in edited form in *MIMAR 39*, Apr-Jun 1991, pp.26-33

[4] Taylor, Brian Brace in the introduction to *Mimar Houses*, AKAA/Concept Media, Singapore, Oct 1987, pp.6-8.

[5] Waterson, Roxana. *The Living House*, Oxford University Press, 1990, p.xv and p.xvii. Dr Waterson lectures in the Faculty of Arts and Social Sciences at the National University of Singapore.

[6] Papanek, Victor in a review of Paul Oliver's "Dwellings: The House across the World", *MIMAR 29*, Sep 1988, pp.76-77.

[7] Papanek, Victor.Ibid

[8] Karogi, Kamau speaking at an Aga Khan Award for Architecture regional seminar in Zanzibar (1988). Recorded in *The Architecture of Housing*, Aga Khan Award for Architecture, Geneva, Nov 1990.

[9] Jencks, Charles. *The New Moderns*, Academy Edition, London, 1990.

[10] Taylor, Brian Brace. Ibid.

[11] Lewcock, Ronald in *The Architecture of Housing*, Aga Khan Award for Architecture, Geneva, Nov 1990.

[12] Serageldin, Ismail. Ibid.

[13] Tay, Kheng Soon. 'Wah so Obiang one', *Straits Times*, Singapore, 28 Mar 1990.

Obiang refers to "someone who is the epitome of bad taste – meaning outdated, cheap, imitative and plastic". The phrase was originally recorded in *Made in Singapore* by Pat Wong, KK Seet and Corinne Chia. Times Books International, Singapore, 1985.

I. USING VERNACULAR FORMS AND MATERIALS

The Tesoro House.

Vernacular architecture can be defined as architecture which does not employ an academically trained architect, but is handed down from generation to generation by ordinary people. It has been variously referred to as indigenous architecture, folk architecture, traditional architecture, primitive architecture, spontaneous architecture and as 'architecture without architects'.

In various ways the five houses in this section are closely related to the vernacular; indeed the Tesoro Rest House in the Philippines and the Giusti House in Bali were built without architects.

All five houses incorporate a deep awareness of the tropical climate. In the Tesoro, Giusti and Mañosa houses, the principal rooms open out directly into the landscape. In the Tesoro Rest House and the Giusti House, the owners sleep on open decks exposed to the tropical breezes, above floors which allow the updraught of cooling air. The houses rely mainly on natural ventilation, though in all five, one or more rooms are air-conditioned.

All have pitched roofs with wide overhanging eaves, one uses *atap* as a roof covering, one *alang-alang* and another uses wood shingles. Water is shed without the use of gutters. There is thus a close relationship between the houses and their surroundings and nature. Natural materials: timber, rattan, clay tiles, sea shells and bamboo are used extensively. Bobby Mañosa uses his house as a test bed for rethinking traditional technology.

The houses take as their precedence the Filipino *nipa* hut, the Balinese *wantilan*, and the basic Javanese *kampong* house. Three of the houses, whether consciously or subconsciously, embody models of the cosmos. Traditional spatial arrangements with a distinct hierarchy of privacy are evident in four of the houses. Thus the vernacular informs the contemporary domestic architecture of Southeast Asia.

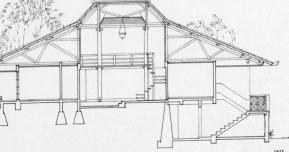

The Sunaryo House.

THE TESORO REST HOUSE

LAGUNA PROVINCE
PHILIPPINES
DESIGNERS: CONRADO A ESCUDERO AND PATIS TESORO
COMPLETED: 1984
EXTENDED: 1987

The house is embraced by dense foliage.

The Tesoro Rest House is in Laguna Province, a two-hour drive from Metro Manila. Patis Tesoro, a highly acclaimed fashion and fabric designer, retreats here at weekends with her lawyer husband Jose Claro Tesoro from their town house in San Juan.

Sited on land which was previously part of the Escudero Estate, the house is surrounded by extensive coconut plantations. The core of the house was created by Conrado 'Ado' Escudero, the indefatigable President of the Villa Escudero Plantations and Resort. Without architectural training but with an instinct for and a knowledge of traditional building forms, he has created a series of wonderful houses in the Laguna area for his family and close friends.

The basic shell is modelled on the traditional *nipa* hut. Ado Escudero paced out a rectangular plan and erected nine circular reinforced concrete 'stilts'. The columns are cast from a reverse mould of a coconut tree, thus the texture replicates the natural form. Patis Tesoro has treated the columns with a terra-cotta paint but in the other houses by Escudero, they are left as raw concrete and they develop a patina which is remarkably natural in appearance and yet allows the concrete to retain its integrity as a man-made material.

The two-storey structure is topped by a high-pitched roof clad in traditional *atap* which projects well beyond the structural frame. At the *sungan* of the roof, *capiz* shell screens emit light onto the soffit of the roof covering and rafters. The upper floor of the main structure is of split bamboo laid on timber joists and is left as an open sleeping deck with the exception of an enclosed space for the Tesoro couple, which is air-conditioned, and a bathroom suite. The lower level has dining, sitting, kitchen and bathroom areas in roughly equal proportions.

The basic house has been subsequently enlarged by Patis Tesoro, firstly by the addition of a two-storey extension which gives space for entertaining and doubles the area of the sleeping deck. A later extension to the side of the structure is a double-height reception/breakfast area which is walled in open rattan screens.

External walls at ground floor level are in woven cane panels set within timber frames. Folding louvred timber doors open out on three sides of the house, directly into the landscaped garden which descends precipitously to a cool mountain stream 20 metres below.

The sound of rushing water, tumbling over rocks is constantly present and at night the family sleeps on the open-sided upper deck with fireflies flickering high in the rafters.

Patis Tesoro like Ado Escudero is an inveterate collector of antique doors and tiles, and the ground floor is finished partly in hand-painted *Machuca* tiles and partly in red clay *Vigan* tiles, which create a pattern interspersed with pebble wash applied to the concrete floor slab.

Embraced by dense foliage, the dwelling is almost impossible to detect from a distance of twenty metres. Sunlight angles through the tree canopy. The 'breathing' external walls allow the owner to commune with nature and the smells and sounds of the plantation to penetrate the house. The house is agreeably cool but occasionally fans are used in the dining room.

The house is simple and yet totally captivating. That it has been 'designed' by two people, neither of whom is an academically trained architect, gives pause for reflection. They have produced a dwelling which touches man's most primordial instinct. It embodies an essential harmony between man and the natural environment, a quality which is timeless.

Second-storey plan.
Plan surveyed by RCP Olavydez.

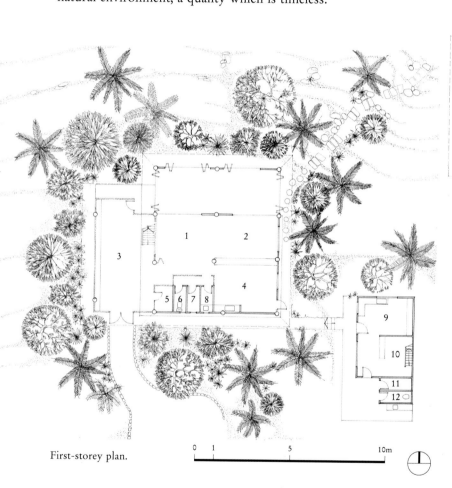

First-storey plan.

0   1   5   10m

1 living area
2 dining area
3 *lanai*
4 auxilliary kitchen
5 store
6 WC
7 shower
8 lavatory
9 dirty kitchen
10 servant's quarter
11 shower
12 WC
13 upper part of *lanai*
14 Sleeping area
15 master bedroom
16 WC
17 shower
18 lavatory

The rattan walls of the *lanai*.

A timber staircase leads to the sleeping deck.

The living area which opens into the garden.

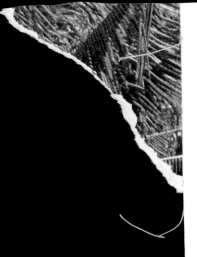

The open-sided sleeping deck.

THE GIUSTI HOUSE

BANJAR SEMAWANG
SANUR . BALI
INDONESIA
DESIGNER: RODOLFO GIUSTI DE MARLE
COMPLETED: 1980

The garden of the Giusti house with the sea beyond.

Rodolfo Giusti's house in Sanur, Bali appropriates some of the traditional patterns of Balinese housing. It sits within a high wall on three sides yet is open to the sea on the east. The visitor enters through an imposing roofed gateway in the southwest corner.

Within the enclosing wall are a series of pavilions which loosely interpret the traditional Balinese house form, although there is no claim to replicate the cosmological and hierarchical relationships of a Balinese family compound. Judged in this light the purist might be overcritical of the European owner's appropriation of forms but nevertheless the house is worthy of further study for its use of traditional materials and proportions.

There are six pavilions within the perimeter wall. The main house, the guest pavilion which also contains an office, the dining area/kitchen, the guardhouse, the garden pavilion and, somewhat pragmatically, a garage pavilion.

Few gardens give as much pleasure as that in the Giusti residence with its sensitively framed views of the ocean. There can be few more exhilarating sights than that of a Bugis trading vessel, on the horizon under full sail, or the reverse view of the house from the beach, framed by waving palm trees, across a reflecting lily pond.

These are romantic notions that the expatriate owner imposes on the traditional arrangement of a Balinese walled compound. A Balinese would probably not open out the house to the sea since *kelod* – the seaward direction is regarded as *Nista* and the repository of evil spirits, within the concept of *Tri Angga* (Budihardjo, 1990).

The main house was built in 1980 and consists of a rectangular first storey of five bays, which supports a similar sized second storey on a combination of coconut timber columns and brick load-bearing walls. The form is a modification of the *wantilan*, a public gathering place. The plan at ground level is completely open with the exception of the southern-most bay. Constructed of brick, and air-conditioned, this bay is used as a repository for books and other objects which would deteriorate in the tropical climate and as guest rooms.

On the upper floor 25 percent of the area is open-to-sky, with a sleeping platform reached by a circular timber staircase. The remainder of the sleeping accommodation is not air-conditioned but has mosquito screens. At the northern end of the house a single room, which protrudes above the roofline, offers a panoramic view of the coastline.

Giusti uses the traditional *alang-alang* roof. An *alang-alang* roof has a life of about twenty to thirty years and, after this period, has to be renewed. In all respects it is excellent. It is well-insulated, waterproof and, if constructed

The form of the Giusti House is a modification of the *Wantilan*.

Above: The roof covering is *alang-alang* using traditional techniques.
Overleaf: The house viewed from the beach. The roof is the
dominant feature.

An open-to-sky sleeping platform at second storey.

properly, does not harbour insects or termites. Moreover it has a natural quality which is impossible to reproduce in clay or concrete. It gives a distinctive roof silhouette that is comfortably embraced within the natural landscape.

The essence of a tropical house is the roof and the manner in which water is shed from the roof. Few dwellings express this with such clarity and honesty as the Giusti House. It springs directly from the vernacular and affirms the resilience of vernacular materials, technology and forms. It links directly with the culture in which it is located.

A tripartite arrangement of *Nista*, *Madya* and *Utama* are evident in the treatment of base, column and roof (Budhihardjo, 1990). The truthful expression of materials is evident as is the clarity of structure.

The owner's fascination with Asian culture is evident from the collection of artifacts and icons. These include stone statues of Lord Shiva, traditional Balinese gongs, Chinese porcelain, marble-topped *kopi tiam* tables, Chinese beds and Balinese carved doors – an array of precious objects that celebrates the depth and richness of Southeast Asian cultures.

The living area opens out on three sides, into the garden.

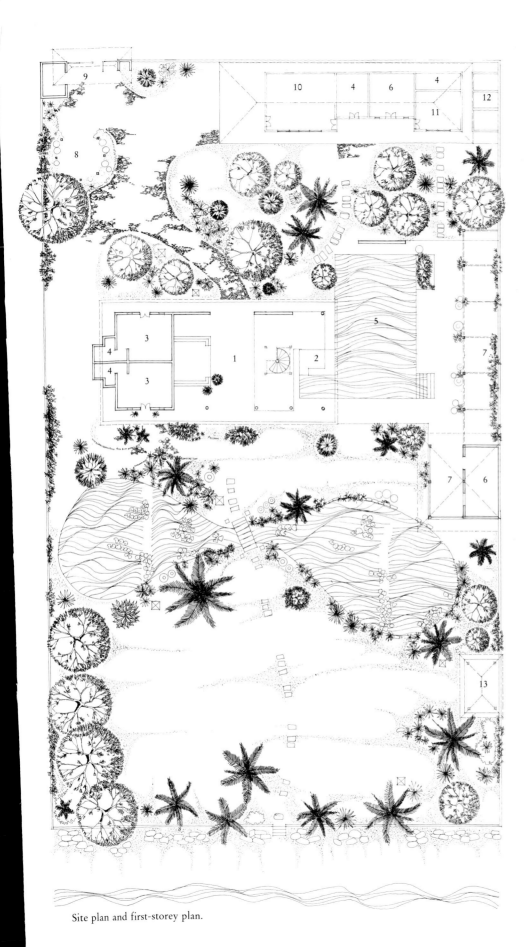

1	living area
2	sunken bar
3	bedroom
4	bathroom
5	pool
6	kitchen
7	dining terrace
8	garage
9	gatehouse
10	office
11	guest room
12	store
13	garden pavilion
14	master bedroom
15	bathroom
16	dressing room
17	sleeping deck

0 1   5   10m

Site plan and first-storey plan.

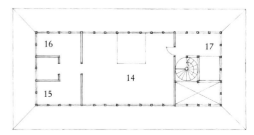

Second-storey plan.

29

BUKIT PAKAR TIMUR
BANDUNG . JAVA
INDONESIA
DESIGNER: SUNARYO
COMPLETED: 1984 (COMMENCED 1975)

Above: The house overlooks the city of Bandung.
Right: The entrance terrace and *serambi*. The stained glass is designed by Sunaryo.

Sunaryo is one of Indonesia's most accomplished contemporary sculptors and painters. He has received no formal training as an architect, but he is responsible for "about 80 percent" of the design of his own house, though he admits to having had assistance in drawing the necessary plans.

Much of the house was built by site instruction. The height of the mezzanine floor level in the centre of the house was spontaneously decided by Sunaryo: "I wanted it to be just so!" he says and jumps to touch the underside of the supporting beam. The human body becomes the measure of the house.

The steps up are not standardised but, "sometimes I want them steep, sometimes shallow – it is a question of feeling what is the right dimension." He gave detailed instructions on site about the placing of round pebbles in the newly laid concrete to achieve a desired texture and demonstrated to the contractor the exact placing of each stone.

Sited high on a hillside, the Sunaryo House overlooks a banana plantation on steep terraces, and has a view to the south, across the city of Bandung to the mountains beyond. The climate in Bandung is more than 5° cooler than that in Jakarta and the air is clearer. A cooling wind blows up the valley and infiltrates through the roof openings and through fanlights over doorways and windows. Air-conditioning is unnecessary – only in one room does the artist use it – where paperwork is kept.

The *parti* for the house is a rectangular plan, divided into nine smaller rectangles. This may have been a sub-conscious reference to known and familiar forms. The raising of the house on a stone podium, which resulted from pragmatic concerns of function, may similarly have been a sub-conscious use of familiar architectural language and proportions.

Sunaryo intended to create a strong base for the house in much the same way that a piece of sculpture needs a base. Then above this the structure could be lighter, with the third horizontal element, the roof, extending as much as 1.8 metres beyond the wall and verandahs.

The artist is articulate about the conscious creation of a hierarchy of privacy. A visitor is made to turn on entering the main gate. Then to turn again to face the main door of the house. A terrace projects in the form of a *serambi*, a seating area for greeting guests.

The nine square plan – a *mandala* – has a sunken central area for the family to gather. Above the central lowered portion is a mezzanine floor which is reserved for family prayers and has a small study, with the corner roof spaces utilised for light storage.

The roof does not have gutters; therefore to reduce the rate of water run off

Terrace with sculpture by Sunaryo.

1 terrace (*teras*)
2 reception area (*galeri*)
3 sunken sitting area (*kamar tamu*)
4 living area (*kamar keluarga*)
5 dining area (*kamar makan*)
6 kitchenette
7 study
8 master bedroom (*kamar tidur utama*)
9 bathroom
10 closet
11 children's bedroom (*kamar anak anak*)
12 studio
13 deck
14 garage (*garasi*)
15 kitchen (*dapur*)
16 maids' room (*kamar pembantu*)
17 utility

from the house, Sunaryo laid coconut fibre mats beneath the open jointed paving to absorb the rain and reduce erosion.

Outdoor areas are designed as a series of platforms for the sculptor's own work – they are set on rock or concrete or timber bases against a backcloth of natural landforms. The artist has added an outdoor working platform to the east elevation of the house and his canvases and sculptural works are everywhere, integrated with the physical structure of the house.

Thought has clearly gone into the natural and artificial lighting of the house. Spotlights highlight paintings and sculpture whilst the setting sun creates a moving pattern of light within the dwelling.

Much of the furniture is Sunaryo's own design, as is the stained glass in the *serambi* and the brass light pendant over the entrance. The house is a work of love and of art. At every turn there is evidence of a thoughtful decision, a conscious sense of proportion, of light, of juxtaposition of materials all within a strong geometric context. It is similar to the artist's recent work 'My Bali'.

The four circular columns supporting the central roof are in straight-grained timber. All walls stop at the underside of the roof truss to assist in cross ventilation. The gap above this level is infilled by open, timber screens. Access to the mezzanine is by carefully detailed timber stairs. The floor finishes indicate certain courses of action and codes of behaviour.

Planting around the house gives a distinctively 'oriental' ambience, with its use of bamboo fences, bamboo groves, circular river-washed boulders and pebbles and soft pink blossoms – in some ways almost Japanese, a feeling which is enhanced by the dark, narrow, horizontal lines on the external white walls. Sunaryo has created a distinctly restful and gentle house which is in harmony with its site.

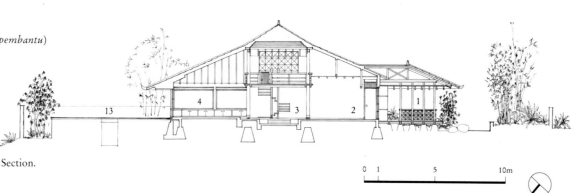

Section.

0　1　　　　5　　　　　10m

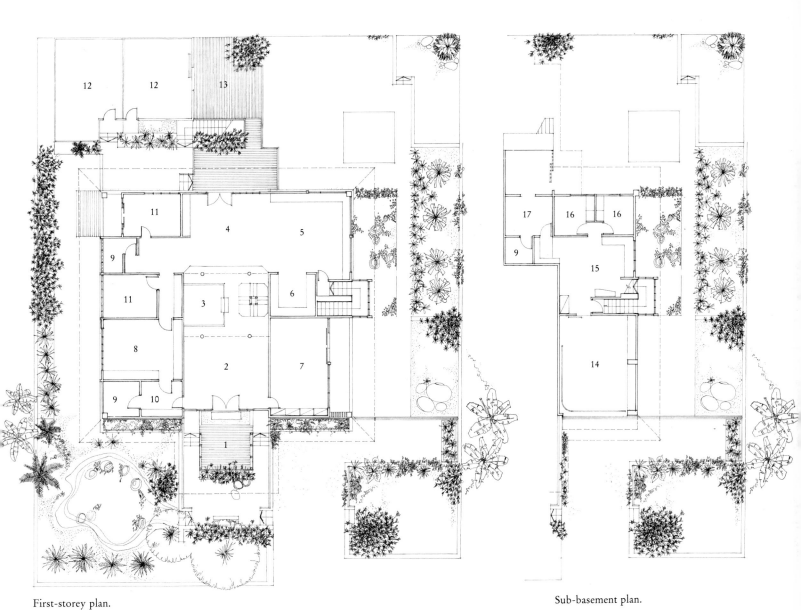

First-storey plan.

Sub-basement plan.

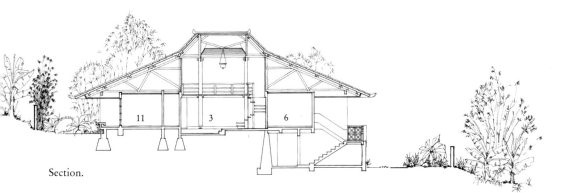

Section.

A timber staircase leads to the mezzanine level.

Above: The reception area. The paintings are by Sunaryo.
Left: The sunken sitting area with dining area beyond.

THE MOERSID HOUSE

JALAN TERATAI
JAKARTA . JAVA
INDONESIA
ARCHITECT: ADHI MOERSID . ATELIER ENAM
COMPLETED: 1975
EXTENDED: 1986

The house embraces an existing tree.

Adhi Moersid, a partner in the highly respected architectural practice Atelier Enam, modestly calls this a "growing house". The 700 square metre site, located within a *kampong* to the south of Jakarta, came into his possession in the mid-1970's. At that time Atelier Enam was a fledgling practice and with limited capital Adhi Moersid embarked on the first stage of a house that has subsequently, like a traditional *kampong* house, been extended several times, the last major addition having been made in 1986.

The architect explains his concept of the house thus: "I started with the basic philosophy of the Javanese traditional house, but I intended that the Javanese qualities should be in the covert aspect of its architecture rather than the overt. It is really a simple low-cost contemporary house, yet I intended that it should have a Javanese atmosphere."

Adhi Moersid, like the Sri Lankan architect Geoffrey Bawa, shows an instinctive sensibility to the site – the house embraces a tree and has the hallmark of every 'good' tropical house: it is designed in such a way that air-conditioning is almost unnecessary. The main living areas do not even employ ceiling fans, yet they are quite comfortable even at the hottest time of the year in May/June, due to the openness of the external walls and the cross ventilation achieved by the linear plan arrangement. The gateway to the house is in the northeast corner. Existing trees have been retained and the entrance and carport are tight against the site boundary.

The entrance area reveals the owner's cultural sensibilities. It is designed with a chest high wall defining the space. Built-in seating runs along two walls and three steps ascend to the next level of privacy. This change of floor level indicates to the visitor that beyond is private space and one should not proceed without invitation.

A mere acquaintance or a casual visitor will naturally stop here – space is defined and hierarchy is clear. This is the area for refreshments to be served and/ or conversation with a visitor. Ascending the three steps to the dining area is an important threshold. One enters into the 'family' area; to sit at the family table. It is an important distinction and the architecture signifies this threshold clearly but with subtlety.

The house is single storey with a very high ceiling which has exposed timber roof rafters. In the gable ends there are ventilation gaps and thus warm air escapes at roof level. The ventilation openings also create a mellow quality of top light which accentuates the height of the main family rooms.

The original house was compactly planned incorporating two bedrooms and a bathroom and an economically sized kitchen. The first of several exten-

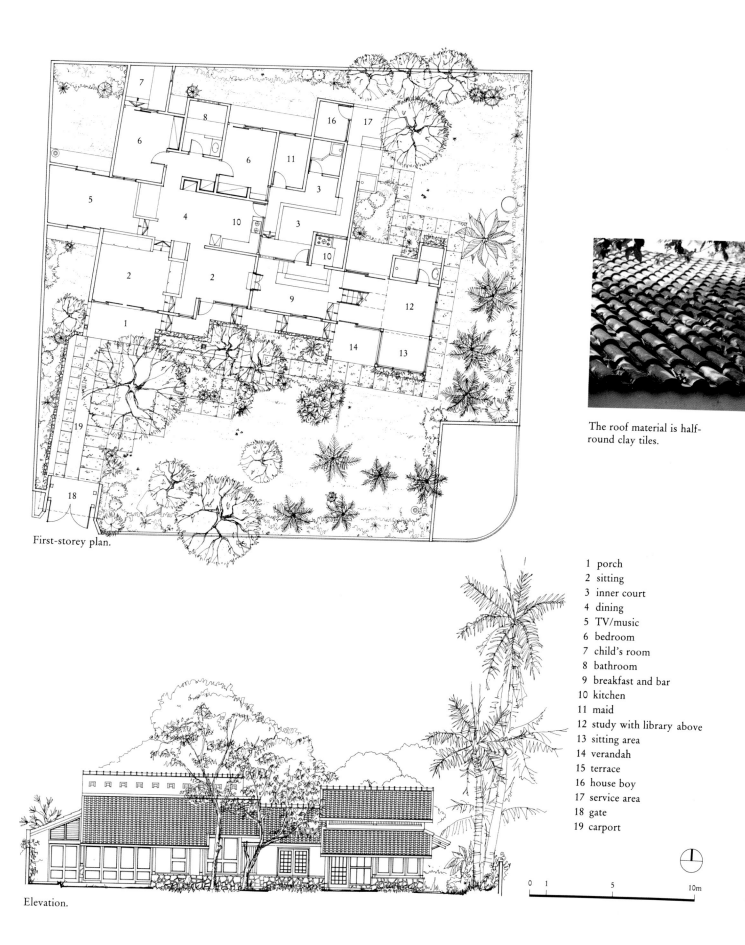

First-storey plan.

The roof material is half-round clay tiles.

Elevation.

1 porch
2 sitting
3 inner court
4 dining
5 TV/music
6 bedroom
7 child's room
8 bathroom
9 breakfast and bar
10 kitchen
11 maid
12 study with library above
13 sitting area
14 verandah
15 terrace
16 house boy
17 service area
18 gate
19 carport

0 1   5   10m

sions enlarged the usable area and incorporated a traditional carved door with a raised threshold. Subsequent extensions have created a design studio for Ananda Moersid who lectures in interior design, and a mezzanine level with library. The 1986 addition incorporates a verandah overlooking the garden. The human scale of the building is enhanced by bringing the eaves very low – less than two metres above external ground level. There are no gutters.

Materials are plastered brickwork (originally fair faced), timber and cement tiles. The kitchen is of modest size and does not boast the array of labour-saving devices we now come to regard as 'necessities'. The architectural composition is complemented and enhanced by several works of art and artifacts from Java and elsewhere in Indonesia. The emphasis the architect/owner confirms is on simplicity and naturalness.

The house has almost reached its ultimate expansion and any further growth will presumably be of a minor nature. The whole dwelling is a subtle recollection of Javanese *kampong* culture, designed with an unerring grasp of qualities of materials.

The house has been extended several times.

The sitting area with dining area beyond.

Breakfast area and bar.

THE MAÑOSA HOUSE

ALABANG . MANILA
PHILIPPINES
ARCHITECT: FRANCISCO 'BOBBY' MAÑOSA
COMPLETED: 1982

Stone steps ascend to the entrance.

The traditional *nipa* hut provides the point of departure for the design concept of the Mañosa House. Bobby Mañosa was named in 1982 as one of the seven visionary architects of Asia[1] and his design philosophy and guiding principles are generated by a desire to create a Philippine identity in architecture. Thus the return to the *bahay kubo* and a sustained investigation of the technical properties of local materials: volcanic rock, volcanic ash, bamboo, coconut, sea shells, timber, rock, banana leaves, rattan, clay and fossilised stone. The greatest difficulty he has faced in his pioneering work with these products has been to gain their acceptance by sceptical clients and fellow architects, for they are regarded by many as fit only for the houses of fishermen or peasant farmers.

The Mañosa House designed in collaboration with his wife Denise, is a blend of Philippine materials and crafts with contemporary lifestyle. The form of their home is basically two squares. The larger of the two has a high-pitched double roof and wide overhanging eaves. The roof is finished with wood shingles made from 30% coconut tree trunk and 70% *apitong*.

Family life revolves around the high central space, square on plan, beneath the apex of the main roof. From the junction of the four principal structural members of the roof, hangs a magnificent chandelier in black *pen* and *capiz* shells. Clerestory windows just beneath the roof are 'glazed' in coloured *capiz* shells, permitting a gentle quality of light to emphasise the height of the room. The walls of this living space are clad in *narra* wood panels inlaid with black *pen* and mother-of-pearl mouldings.

This central living space is flanked on two sides to a wide *balconaje*. The walls of this verandah are permanently open and the roof overhangs are supported by inclined struts which are an interpretation of the *tukod* (supports) of the *nipa* hut windows.

The roof extension is brought down low to align with the horizon and thus eliminate glare. Around the perimeter of the balcony is a continuous bench seat combined with a balcony rail. The floor of the *balconaje* is of *molave* and coco wood strips.

Much of the family activities take place in this space, which is naturally ventilated. The rafters and purlins are revealed beneath the high sloping roof and suspended fans assist in air movement on sultry evenings. There are a number of 'conversation areas' on the balcony with flexible grouping of chairs and tables.

At one end of the L-shaped balcony is a bar, the ceiling of which is clad in coconut shell laminates. At the other end is a glass-walled video and TV room which is air-conditioned. The wide screen equipment can be viewed from

Elevation.

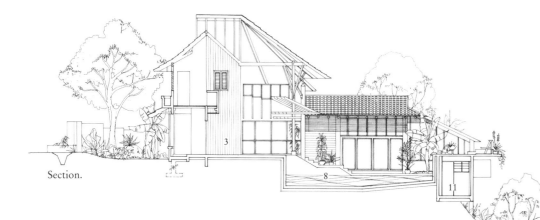

Section.

Looking from the gallery to distant views of forested hills.

62

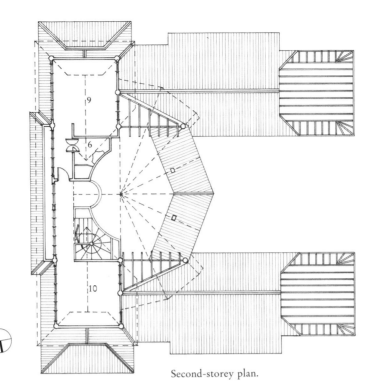

1 garage
2 entry
3 living
4 kitchen
5 maids' room
6 washing
7 sleeping
8 swimming pool
9 guest room
10 den/gallery
11 pump room
12 drive

0 1   5   10m

Second-storey plan.

First-storey plan.

Malaysia, turns this to advantage – his detailing is sturdy and inventive. It contrasts with the delicate Thai hand-carved doors.

Both of Jimmy Lim's houses illustrated in this book, which so enchantingly capture the essence of traditional Malay architecture and translate it into a modern form, are owned by or occupied by Europeans. The architect is brutally frank in his assertion that many Malaysians "do not know how to live graciously. Anything that is Western is felt by many educated Malaysians to be good, anything that is traditional is felt to be backward". It is a notion that the architect seeks through his work to overturn and he has been fortunate in the last decade to have had a fairly constant flow of local and foreign clients who share his belief.

The radiating timber roof structure.

Above: The living area and walled garden beyond.
Right: The gallery overlooks the double-height living area.

THE WONG HOUSE

LEEDON ROAD
SINGAPORE
ARCHITECT: WILLIAM LIM ASSOCIATES
COMPLETED: 1991

The built form is in harmony with the landscape.

When the owners of this house purchased the site on Leedon Road, it contained an existing rectangular-shaped bungalow with a double-pitched roof. The instruction was to extend the house incorporating modern conveniences without losing its "traditional feeling". The brief required the house to be of low profile and not unnecessarily ostentatious. Perhaps this expresses an attitude to life.

One of the constraints facing the architect was that the existing bungalow was situated in the very centre of the site. This has been turned to advantage and the private functions of the house are incorporated into a new extension at the rear of the site.

The extension and the remodelled existing building are separated by and overlook a small fish pond. This open-to-sky space is the heart of the dwelling – here the family take breakfast or dine privately overlooking the pond, accompanied by the gentle sound of a splashing fountain. If a larger dinner party is in progress, the guests move from the reception hall and bar area to dine formally at a table alongside the pond.

One major change to the existing building was the stripping out of the ceiling, which raised the apparent height of the central reception hall, and exposed the timber roof structure and the space between rafters which has been re-lined with timber boarding. It is a restful space with efficient cross ventilation from the prevailing breezes through large openings. There is no air-conditioning in the reception hall; it relies on natural air movement supplemented by ceiling fans.

The dwelling embodies a traditional Chinese hierarchical arrangement of functions with distinct thresholds between the most public areas and the most private. A party can be held without any necessity for guests to go into the private/family domain of the house.

The new extension at the rear of the site consists of a two-storey building which houses the breakfast room and the European-style kitchen on the first storey and the master bedroom above. The breakfast room is the centre for family activities and a place which attracts family members to sit and read by the open window overlooking the fish pond. To the rear of the house in a single-storey abutment is the domestic staff room and an 'Asian' kitchen. This single storey returns around the east end to form the family/TV room.

Both teenage children are given a degree of autonomy; they are allocated a separate wing. The architect has separated the family route into the private areas from a service route which would allow a dinner party to be served directly from the kitchen.

The project architect was Ho Sweet Woon, a graduate of the National

University of Singapore. Later the project was taken over by Lim Cheng Kooi, a graduate from Universiti Teknologi Malaysia. The practice of William Lim Associates has acquired a considerable reputation as a 'nurturer' of young talented designers. The natural features of the site: the surrounding trees and a gentle fall across the site, have been enhanced with sensitive landscaping by Sim Kern Teck. The built form too is in harmony with the natural land form.

This project raises some interesting questions, for William Lim Associates have been associated with some of most avante-garde buildings in Singapore in the last decade – buildings such as Tampines North Community Centre and Church of Our Saviour, as well as Kuala Lumpur's Central Square development in Malaysia – yet here we see a gradually developing thesis which is remarkably different. The concern here is with the transformation of the vernacular architectural tradition into a modern residence. Experience shows that this is what most people are comfortable with – why for example are Frank Lloyd Wright's and Geoffrey Bawa's houses so timeless?

What is more, houses such as the Wong House utilise the tropical climate, are not wasteful of resources; they are in harmony with the land, are a link with and part of an evolving tradition, and they are culturally conscious artifacts.

The Wong House has a low profile and is unostentatious.

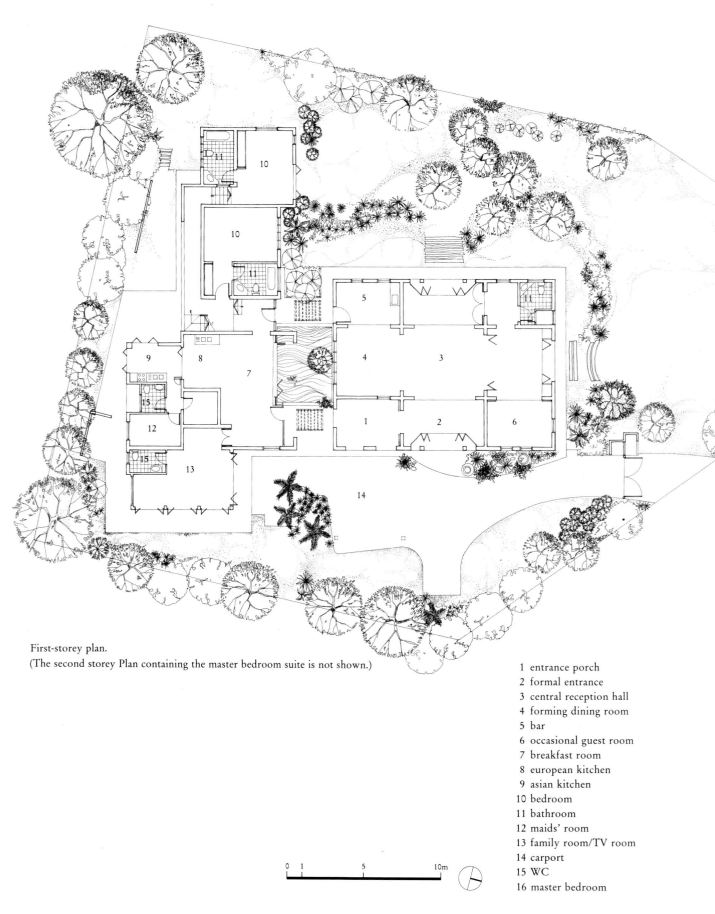

First-storey plan.
(The second storey Plan containing the master bedroom suite is not shown.)

0 1   5   10m

1 entrance porch
2 formal entrance
3 central reception hall
4 forming dining room
5 bar
6 occasional guest room
7 breakfast room
8 european kitchen
9 asian kitchen
10 bedroom
11 bathroom
12 maids' room
13 family room/TV room
14 carport
15 WC
16 master bedroom

Section.

Elevation.

Section.

The central reception hall with exposed roof structure.

The family/TV room with louvred doors on three sides which open into the garden.

A small fish pond is at the heart of the dwelling.

THE INDRA ABIDIN HOUSE

JL PAHLABUTAN
JAKARTA . JAVA
INDONESIA
ARCHITECT: ISMETH ABIDIN
COMPLETED: 1988 (COMMENCED 1985)

Above: The family area has no external walls and opens directly into the garden. Right: The central lightwell and ramp.

Many of the most beautiful urban houses in Southeast Asia give little indication of their true qualities from the street. Frequently they display a modest exterior; this modesty may be a purely pragmatic decision, since to display wealth is to invite intruders, or it may be a deeper cultural response in indigenous cultures. The initial impression of the Abidin House is of an ordinary street facade revealing little of the social status of the owners.

When Indra Abidin decided to build his house in the early 1980's, the conceptual idea was that it should bring together some of the characteristics of his birthplace in Southern Sumatra and those of his wife's in West Java. He is one of Indonesia's foremost graphic designers, she a biologist. The design of the house was entrusted to the client's brother, architect Dr Ismeth Abidin.

The *parti* for the house is a twelve metre by twelve metre square; a *mandala* of nine, four metre by four metre squares. The choice of this module was a pragmatic decision to use a steel structural frame and to optimise on readily available lengths of 'I' section.

Subconsciously the architect created a cosmic symbol with, at its centre, a lofty glazed atrium and a ramp ascending through three storeys. Ismeth Abidin creates a 'processional route' through the house which has a similar purpose to the staircase in the Eu House by Jimmy Lim in Kuala Lumpur. It orchestrates and choreographs the spatial experiences within the house. The centre acts as a constant reference. The central atrium is the heart of the house. It permits filtered sunlight to penetrate into the core of the dwelling.

The square form topped by a pyramidal roof and the use of rich colours – gold, red and bronze, has precedence in Sumatra. From West Java comes the precedence for the still pool of water by the entrance and the changes of level, which indicate a distinct socio-spatial hierarchy in the house. These are juxtaposed with other cultural artifacts – a *pendopo* carved in Kudus, the traditional bed made in Madura and the main entrance door carved in Bali.

One enters the house through a modest street entrance. There is deliberate diminishing of scale; a narrow bridge over a pool focuses attention on an inner ornamentally carved door. One hesitates; the instinctive response is to remove one's shoes. A step up signifies that one is entering a domain where certain behaviour is expected.

Beyond the entrance with its pool there is an change of scale, an expansive gesture of a high central atrium signifying 'welcome'. One descends into an airy, spacious three-storey-high living and dining area which opens out directly to an enclosed garden with a high wall covered in foliage. The traditional *pendopo*, is located at the rear of the house.

The studio with the ramp beyond.

There are no solid walls in the rear of the house – improbable as it may seem, the whole house is enclosed in a steel mesh box; the mesh provides a frame for plants and it appears totally transparent whilst giving security.

The spatial hierarchy continues vertically. A short ramp leads to a more private level – open but less accessible. Here is a prayer area for the head of the family. There is also a study area and a private library. Ascending further is a more private family room and at the very highest level there are family bedrooms. The central atrium is roofed with a steel space frame and glazed with the topmost panels of the pyramidal roof inverted to collect water, which is directed down a central rainwater pipe. This pipe has perforations and is surrounded by a wire frame which supports climbing foliage. The plants are thus naturally irrigated and the spray of water that results helps to cool, by evaporation, the interior of the house.

With the exception of the bedrooms the house is naturally ventilated. The openness of the planning creates internal conditions that are not at all uncomfortable. There are some disadvantages living in a house without air-conditioning or fans. Mosquitoes are one difficulty, dampness in clothing and books another and in urban locations dust is a perennial problem. But the Abidin House shows that none of these difficulties outweigh the advantages of a close relationship with nature in a well designed micro-climate.

The house is the product of clients who are dedicated to exploring their cultural origins and a simple, but inspired concept by their architect. Working within the constraints of the materials and available craftsmanship, they have produced a house which goes beyond the functional planning of space and the manipulation of light; a house with the ability to move the spirit.

It is the owner's intention to dismantle and move the whole house to a new site in the future. The house was planned with this in mind and the steel components have all been numbered for the imminent move. This recalls a traditional Indonesian practice of moving houses (see Waterson – *The Living House*, 1987).

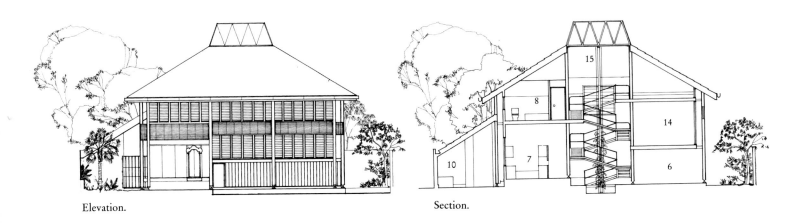

Elevation.   Section.

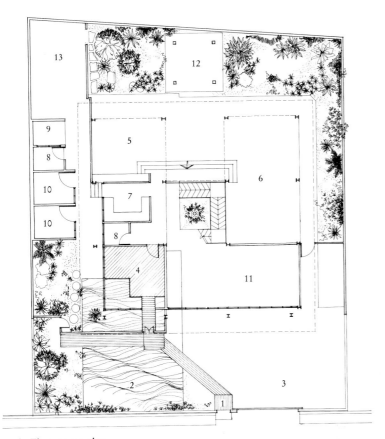

First-storey plan.

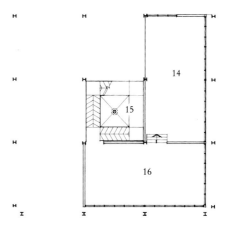

Third-storey plan.

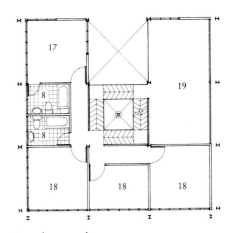

Second-storey plan.

1 gate
2 pond
3 garage (*garasi*)
4 lobby (*lobbi*)
5 dining area (*kamar makan*)
6 family area
7 kitchen (*dapur*)
8 bath/WC
9 service (*cuci*)
10 maid (*kamar pembantu*)
11 storage
12 pavilion
13 drying yard
14 studio
15 central lightwell
16 living room (*kamar keluarga*)
17 master bedroom (*kamar tidur utama*)
18 bedroom (*kamar tidur*)
19 storage (*loteng*)

0 1   5   10m

The family area at first-storey level.

THE TIPTUS HOUSE

BANGKOK
THAILAND
ARCHITECT: BOONYAWAT AND PUSSADEE TIPTUS
COMPLETED: 1983

The entrance porch with verandah above.

The Tiptus House has received considerable acclaim since it was awarded the Association of Siamese Architects under Royal Patronage Gold Medal in 1984. The owners are both architects and they set out to design a house which employed the cost and labour saving technology of concrete prefabrication yet simultaneously embodied the essence of traditional Thai architecture. The result is a seminal dwelling, in which they have jointly invested great care and thought. Architecture is ultimately about an attitude to life and to the relationship with other living things – animals and plants.

It is simple and economical but rich in detail and in harmony with its surroundings. It is a more modest house than many in this book and consequently it conveys a quality of dwelling and of lifestyle that would not be beyond the resources of many first time house builders in the region.

The house is about re-establishing roots – the architects/owners have done much background research into the essence of a tropical house in Thailand and its translation into modern form. The model for the house is the single-storey wooden structure on tall stilts that was the dominant form in the central region of Thailand in the early Rattanakosin period (1782 onwards). This form of traditional Thai house had an elevated wooden verandah and a group of buildings arranged around and on this wooden platform.

Bangkok lies on the principal river of Thailand, the Chao Phrya and, being prone to periodic flooding, the houses of the region were lifted well above the flood level. When the flood subsided the space beneath the deck became a store or a space for working.

The main structure of the traditional Thai house was timber and to this were attached prefabricated panels made of local materials such as thatch, bamboo or flat timber board. The Tiptus House adopts this construction method using modern materials.

Tropical houses always have to contend with very hot sunshine, and frequent rainfall particularly in the monsoon period. Traditionally these would be solved by having a roof with wide overhangs. This became another principal of the Tiptus House, together with the concomitant requirement for cross ventilation and shade.

Finally the traditional Thai house was a manifestation of family relationships and cultural practices. A single-family house usually consisted of more than one dwelling unit. It had a separate sleeping unit for the head of the family, a unit for children, another for living, and others for cooking and storage. These were grouped around the central platform and as a family grew, married sons or daughters would attach additional units to the central platform. Thus the house form reflected living patterns and social relationships.

When the Tiptuses embarked on the design of their house, it was a conscious act of resistance to the intrusion of "international style" architecture into Thai culture. They set out to synthesise the design principles of the traditional Thai house in terms of atmosphere and spacial relationships with modern technology.

To respond to the tropical climate most areas in the house are orientated towards the prevailing south and southwesterly winds. The separation of the house into smaller units facilitates the flow of wind. By locating the house on the north part of the site, space has been created for a water-filled pond on the southern half of the site – this is intended to cool the breezes and it appears to be effective. The house is designed with overhangs, which shade windows and walls. A trellis covers the communal terrace over which flowering shrubs grow, thus creating a shaded and fragrant environment. Fibre glass insulation is placed within the east and west wall construction to reduce heat gain on those elevations most exposed to the sun.

Site plan.

The house viewed from the garden at night.

Section.

Section.

A pergola shades the roof terrace.

1 living area	11 fish pond
2 dining room	12 master bedroom (parent unit)
3 antique store	13 children's unit
4 terrace	14 study room
5 pantry	15 bedroom
6 kitchen	16 living unit
7 laundry	17 verandah
8 maid	18 open well
9 storage	19 roof garden
10 parking	

0 1   5   10m

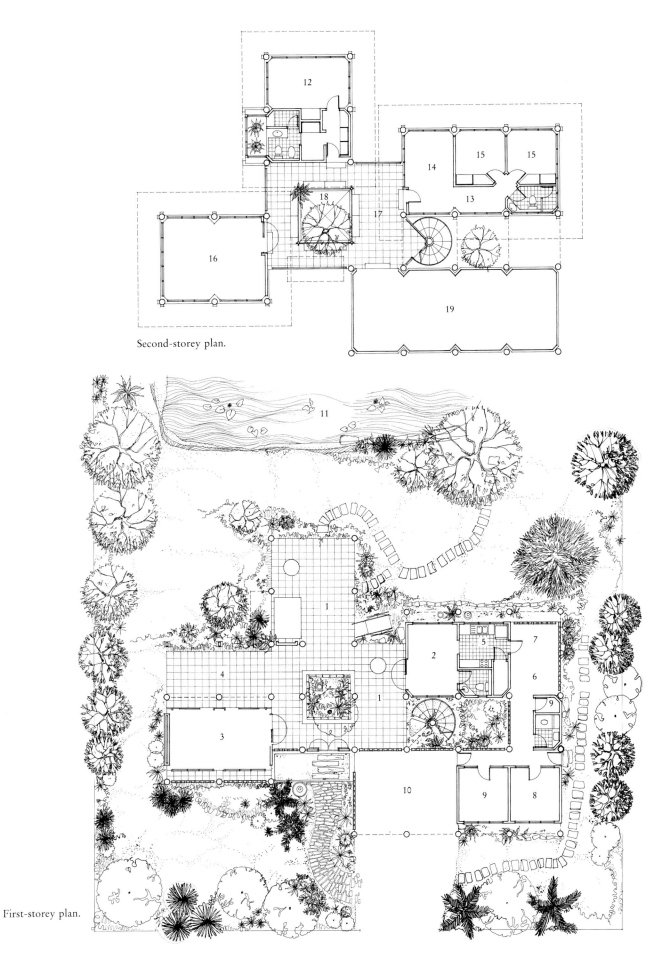

Second-storey plan.

First-storey plan.

Privacy is created by adopting the traditional spatial hierarchy. The house thus has separate units for the parents, the children, for living (eg. listening to music, reading, socialising) and for cooking. Outdoor and semi-outdoor spaces are utilised for relaxation, for receiving friends and entertaining guests. The sleeping units are designed as strictly functional minimal areas.

The architects have used their house to explore and research their ideas on the use of low-cost materials. The *in situ* concrete frame of the house was constructed using only two moulds whilst the precast concrete beams and floor units are rationalised to a simple module. Handmade sun-dried bricks, terracotta and glazed ceramic tiles are incorporated into the house. Walls are prefabricated within a wooden frame, in much the same way that prefabricated panels were used in the past.

One concession to modern technology is the use of a flat concrete roof behind a pitched perimeter section. This is to provide space for an array of solar collectors and an air-conditioning compressor which would sit uncomfortably on a traditional high pitched roof.

The house is a rigorous exploration of how vernacular and modern technology can be synthesised. It is a beautiful contemporary dwelling closely related to the site and in harmony with nature.

A construction detail.

The living area and open light-well.

The house viewed from the garden pavilion.

The small fish pond and garden pavilion.

THE BIN TONG PARK HOUSE

SINGAPORE
ARCHITECT: ERNESTO BEDMAR . BEDMAR AND SHI
COMPLETED: 1991

Above: The portico with tall brick-faced columns.
Right: The house viewed from the entrance gate.

Beautiful residences are often disarmingly simple in concept and this is the case with the Bin Tong Park residence; it has clarity and precision and yet a delightful informality. At the heart of the house is a two-storey-high gallery and reception space with exposed timber roof trusses. The major rooms open off this central atrium which has a northwest facing, glazed wall, protected from the setting sun by a two-storey-high portico.

The tall, brick-faced columns of the portico give the house a slightly monumental quality, which is offset by two single-storey pavilions that project forward from the rectangular main block to enclose a landscaped court.

The designer of the house, which is owned by a Singaporean Chinese family, is Ernesto Bedmar. The Argentinian born Bedmar studied art in the USA, and architecture under Miguel Angel Roco in Argentina, before moving to Southeast Asia via Hong Kong. The practice of Bedmar and Shi was set up in Singapore in 1987 and now has a number of completed residential projects in Kuala Lumpur and Singapore, the hallmark of which is "understated elegance".

Bedmar's formative years in South America, his exposure to American design and his subsequent working experience in Hong Kong and Macau, bring an international dimension to the work of the practice. At the same time, Bedmar has also absorbed the traditional responses to climate and culture in Southeast Asia.

The house functions well, even without the central air-conditioning which is provided. The northwest portico has four large, centre-pivot, glazed doors which can be angled to catch the breezes. The lounge area opens out through folding, glazed doors onto a timber deck. This overlooks a walled garden at the rear of the house, with a fish pond and a fountain. The pond cools the southeast facing terrace and the sound of running water soothes the spirit.

Harmony between the inside and the outside of the house is achieved through close cooperation between the architect and the Bali-based landscape designer Michael White, who incorporates a number of rock features, Balinese carvings and huge water jars into the garden.

The house is on slightly elevated land and, from the larger of the two pavilions, the owners can look to the northwest and to the west towards a tree-fringed horizon. This open pavilion has built-in furniture and is naturally ventilated. The smaller pavilion houses the family cars and gives access into the two-storey main house or, via the covered portico, to the open pavilion.

The double-height reception gallery is a dramatic space which, during parties held by the owner, naturally becomes the space to which guests gravitate. The open-plan interior allows for flexibility in the use of spaces.

Bedmar uses materials as truthfully as permitted by stringent Singapore building regulations. The twin columns of the pavilion which appear to be timber have a core of structural steel. The house has a rich ambience, with its clay-tiled floor and rough textured Malaccan brick, capped by stained timber trusses and red 'Marseilles' roof tiles. The ground floor is finished in 300 millimetre square Cantonese terracotta tiles. Antique carpets are strategically placed and in the dining room the floor changes to teak timber boarding.

Roofs shed water into storm drains at ground level. The sound of water is one of the qualities of tropical architecture which sets it apart from that of other climatic regions.

The owners' lifestyle, their frequent entertaining, their love of music and art are accommodated comfortably. Although this is a big house (945 square metres), it retains the 'homely' atmosphere that Ernesto Bedmar strives for in his domestic projects. The house was designed without preconceptions of form or style, but as a response to functional requirements of the owners, and with the intention of visually linking the internal spaces with the exterior.

The outdoor living room overlooks a beautifully landscaped court.

Above: The smaller of two pavilions houses the family cars.   Right: Visitors enter a two-storey high gallery and reception space.

Section.

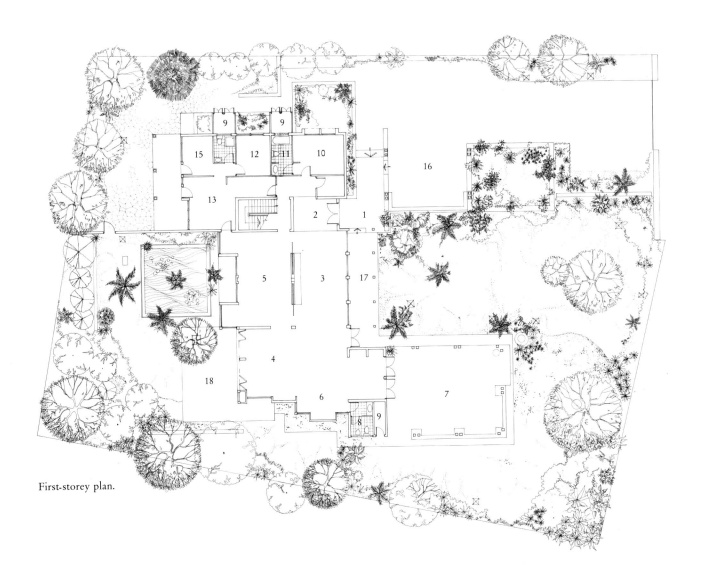

First-storey plan.

Elevation.

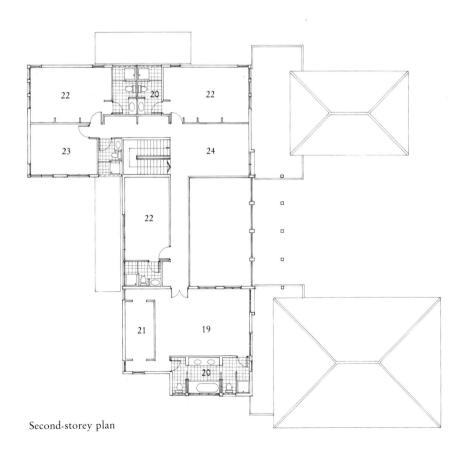

Second-storey plan

1 entrance porch
2 entry hall
3 garden
4 living room
5 dining room
6 bar
7 outdoor living room
8 WC
9 store
10 guest room/TV room
11 bathroom
12 maids' room
13 European kitchen
14 Asian kitchen
15 utility
16 carport
17 terrace
18 wood deck
19 master bedroom
20 bathroom
21 walk-in closet
22 bedroom
23 study
24 family hall

The dining room with the bar beyond.

The open plan of the first storey seen from the bar.

The living area with a floor of Cantonese terracotta tiles.

THE LOCSIN HOUSE

FORBES PARK
MAKATI . METRO MANILA
PHILIPPINES
ARCHITECT: LEANDRO V LOCSIN
COMPLETED: 1963 (ORIGINAL HOUSE)
EXTENDED: 1983 (MUSIC ROOM)

The house viewed from the swimming pool.

The Locsin House is in the exclusive Forbes Park district of Makati. The major part of the house was completed in 1963, but the 1983 addition of a music room blends comfortably with the earlier building to create a 'timeless' work of art embodying continuity and change. The plan is in the form of an 'E' facing away from the public road. Over the central area of the plan is a traditional high-pitched roof, with overhangs of two metres on all sides. Beneath this roof is a double-height living area.

The elevation facing the road is without openings, apart from the centrally positioned carved timber entrance doors, which were recovered from the portals of a seventeenth-century cathedral in Cebu. This solid wall reduces heat gain from the afternoon sun and affords protection from the typhoons which periodically sweep across the country.

Passing through the entrance doors, the visitor crosses a bridge over a rectangular pool, filled with carp and fringed by weeping willows and tropical plants. To the right, a door gives access to a lobby leading to the study and the bedroom wing; to the left, another door opens to a corridor leading to the service wing.

Directly ahead is the reception lobby and beyond this the main living spaces. The floor material changes to polished granite blocks. They originally came to the Philippines from southern China as ballast in old trading vessels. One walks on a surface which carries memories of the route by which Locsin's ancestors arrived in the Philippines in the mid-eighteenth century.

The living area is separated from the dining room by a sliding panel made of translucent *capiz* shells set in a timber frame. This material is used elsewhere; in screens which can be drawn across the fine mesh mosquito screens overlooking the garden, and in the high gables of the traditional roof form, to emit a gentle light which illuminates the timber ceiling.

Water is used within the living area alongside the garden wall. A shallow stream of water runs over dark grey pebbles into a pool. The temperature of the room is thus cooled by evaporation and the micro-climate supports the growth of orchids and ferns.

Wall surfaces in the living and dining areas are of dressed volcanic *tuff* known as *adobe*. The earthy-brown coloured soft rock is found locally in Manila. Lattice-arched screens in the living room are inspired by plantation houses. Here they reduce the glare from rooflights over the indoor garden.

Architect Locsin and his wife Cecelia Yulo, who is an archaeologist, are prolific collectors of oriental ceramics and the basement of their home is a setting for the display of these ceramics and their collection of Philippine religious art.

The two-storey-high living room with dining room beyond.

The arched screens are inspired by plantation houses.

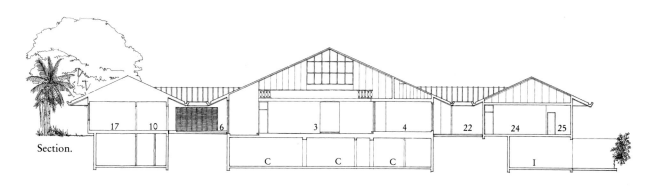

Section.

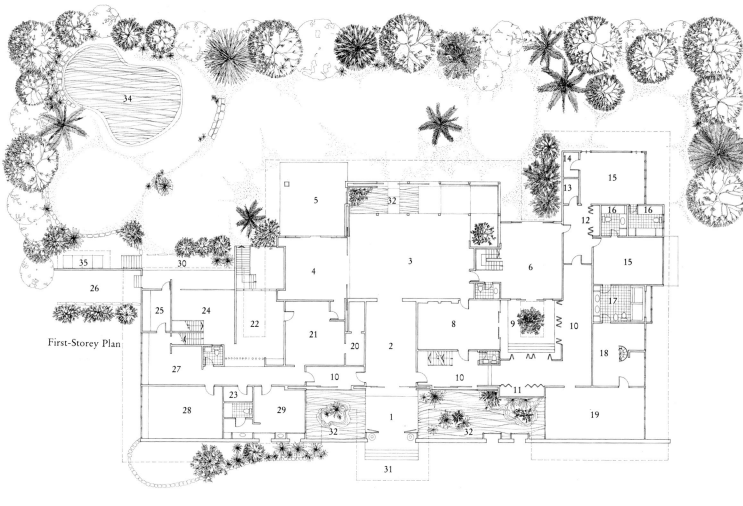

First-Storey Plan

1	entry bridge	13	storage	25	laundry room
2	reception lobby	14	walk-in closet	26	laundry yard
3	living room	15	bedroom	27	utility
4	dining room	16	bathroom	28	maids' quarters
5	*lanai*	17	master bathroom	29	office
6	music room	18	dressing room	30	herb garden
7	powder room	19	master bedroom	31	porch
8	library	20	pantry	32	carp pond
9	inner court	21	kitchen	33	interior wet garden
10	foyer	22	patio	34	swimming pool
11	altar	23	glass/silver store	35	kennels
12	kitchenette	24	service kitchen		

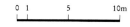

The dwelling is a repository of historical treasures, many integrated into the architecture. The library walls are made of eighteenth-century bricks, recovered from a church destroyed by bombing in World War II. They are laid with narrow mortar joints and create a wonderful textured surface. The library doors are timber bas-relief panels from a seventeenth-century Cebu cathedral, and the *molave* timber balustrade on the mezzanine above the living area was an altar rail which had been discarded from a cathedral in Batangas.

Leandro (Lindy) Locsin is the Philippines' most venerated architect of the post-war period and his completed projects, which span over 35 years of practice, have "put an indelible stamp on Philippine architecture" (Polites 1977).[1] Locsin is responsible for many of the major buildings in his native country since he came to prominence in 1955, with his design for the Chapel of the Holy Sacrifice. Projects which have brought him international acclaim are the Cultural Centre of the Philippines, the Philippines International Convention Centre and the Philippine Pavilion at Expo 70. All are strongly influenced by the masters of the Modern Movement: Corbusier and Mies van der Rohe, and by Eero Saarinen and Paul Rudolph, whose textured concrete surfaces are much admired by Locsin.

In his residence he fuses the Philippine building traditions: wide overhanging eaves, large roof, interior trellises and spacious, open 'plantation house' ambience with modern technology, in the form of exposed aggregate concrete and wide span beams, to create a 'hybrid'.

It is a beautiful dwelling by one of Asia's greatest modern architects, who seeks to find "the elusive Filipino soul in architecture" (Locsin 1964 and quoted in Klassen 1986).[2]

The basement houses a private museum.

---

[1] Politics, Nicholas in *The Architecture of Leandro V Locsin*, Weatherhill, Tokyo, 1977.
[2] Kassen, *Winand. Architecture in the Philippines*, University of San Marcos, Cebu, Philippines, 1986.

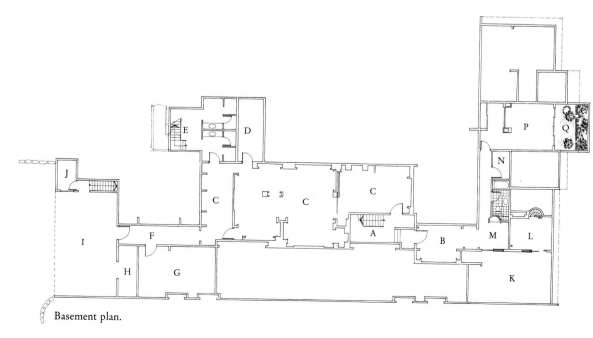

Basement plan.

A   lower foyer
B   celadon room
C   private museum
D   storage
E   pool changing
F   hall
G   storage
H   carpenter shop
I   garage
J   drive
K   study
L   lower dressing room
M   guest
N   sauna
P   guest room
Q   Japanese garden

III. INCORPORATING COLONIAL INFLUENCES

Reuter House.

The colonial influence in Southeast Asia enters the discourse on contemporary houses in the form of the Reuter House in Singapore and the Gunawan House in Jakarta.

The former evokes memories of the 'black and white' bungalows erected by the British, and the latter surfaces memories of the Dutch plantation bungalow.

This is not accidental. In both cases the designers felt the precedence was appropriate. The black and white houses were themselves the product of a synthesis between the Malay *kampong* house and the English Tudor cottage. The British colonists borrowed freely from the vernacular and incorporated high roofs, cross ventilation, raised living areas on stilts or columns, and verandahs with wide overhanging roofs. The timber frame was highlighted in the manner of an English villa and an entrance porch was added for the carriage and later the car. Similarly the Dutch plantation bungalow incorporated a wide verandah space borrowed from the vernacular houses.

In the two houses in this chapter, there is a further synthesis of the colonial house form with modern requirements and technology.

Another colonial house 'type' was the detached villa which borrowed freely from Palladio and which was usually well-adapted to tropical conditions, often borrowing elements from the vernacular Malay house. In recent years there has been a rash of Post-Modern Classicism in the cities of Southeast Asia and a reappearance of this type. Sadly for the most part the proportions of elements in the recent manifestations look distinctly odd to an eye used to the Italian or North European original. In the process of changing the construction technology from stone to concrete, a freedom of expression creeps in which distorts the original, and not always for the better. No contemporary Post-Modern Classical house was considered worthy of inclusion.

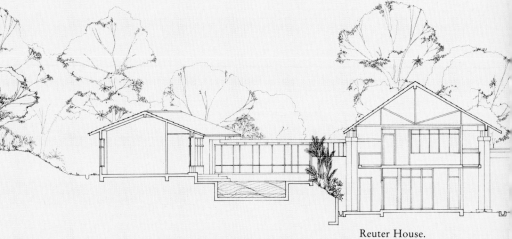

Reuter House.

THE REUTER HOUSE

RIDOUT ROAD
SINGAPORE
ARCHITECT: WILLIAM LIM ASSOCIATES
COMPLETED: 1990

The detailed junction of the roof structure and supporting column.

The plan form of the Reuter House is a rough approximation of the large 'black and white' mansions of the colonial period. That is to say – there is a squarish 'front' block connected to a rectangular rear block via a sheltered and covered walkway or corridor. In a past era, the front block would have been the family residence of the owner, whilst the rear block would have housed kitchens and servant's quarters. In the Reuter House the architect almost reverses these functions – the rear block becomes the private family domain, separated by an open court and swimming pool from the reception rooms, dining area and the more public domain of the house. The kitchen/utility and servant quarters are contained in a separate service block at an angle to the main block.

Supporting the pyramidal roof of the front block of the house are ten huge circular timber columns. These are made of red *balau* tree trunks, surmounted by black-painted steel capitals supporting the main roof trusses. The association that some people draw from this is with a Chinese temple or old houses in China. One wonders if this association is intended or whether it is a sub-conscious move on the part of the designer. Other observers associate these same columns with the classical porticoes of colonial buildings. These are some of the intriguing semiotic observations that arise when a designer pushes the boundaries of architecture beyond the accepted norms.

The elements of modern architectural language that enter the discourse are evident in the fragmentation of the brief. The expression of the brief on plan is as subtly related but clearly articulated separate blocks which have an affinity with the architecture of Frank Gehry.

The front block of the house is disarmingly simple at a first reading, but is actually much more complex. The main pyramidal roof, supported on the two-storey high timber columns, projects beyond the core of the house. It floats like a pavilion, in the manner of the best vernacular tropical architecture. It sheds rain directly to the ground where there are storm drains.

Set within the perimeter columns is an inner concrete structure. This structure is articulated most clearly on the west facade. The expression of the floor slab, open stair well and vertical partition walls is in a modernist language.

Within this is yet a third layer, a lightly framed, square, timber element with glazed walls, all of which can be opened to allow cross ventilation; to allow the room to 'breathe' like the traditional *kampong* house. This square is rotated within the main rectangle, thus on the first floor a rhomboid-shaped verandah is created on the west side, to enjoy the setting sun filtered by the majestic trees that have been retained around the perimeter of the site.

The geometry of the inner square sets up the alignment for the connecting

The main block of the house is a two-storey pavilion.

Timber columns support the pyramidal roof of the main block.

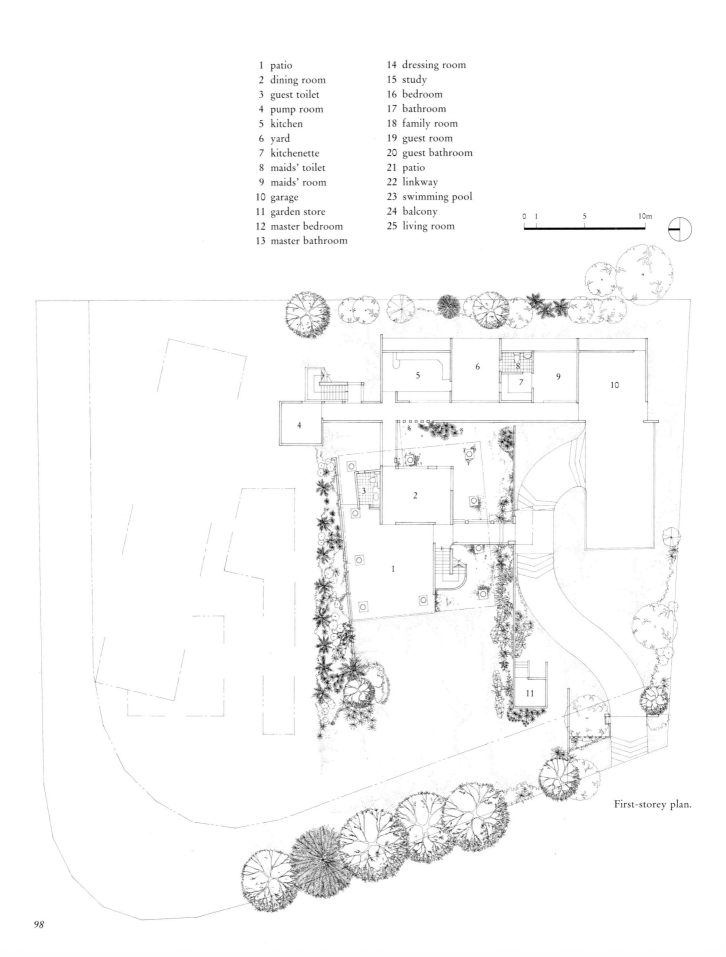

1 patio	14 dressing room
2 dining room	15 study
3 guest toilet	16 bedroom
4 pump room	17 bathroom
5 kitchen	18 family room
6 yard	19 guest room
7 kitchenette	20 guest bathroom
8 maids' toilet	21 patio
9 maids' room	22 linkway
10 garage	23 swimming pool
11 garden store	24 balcony
12 master bedroom	25 living room
13 master bathroom	

First-storey plan.

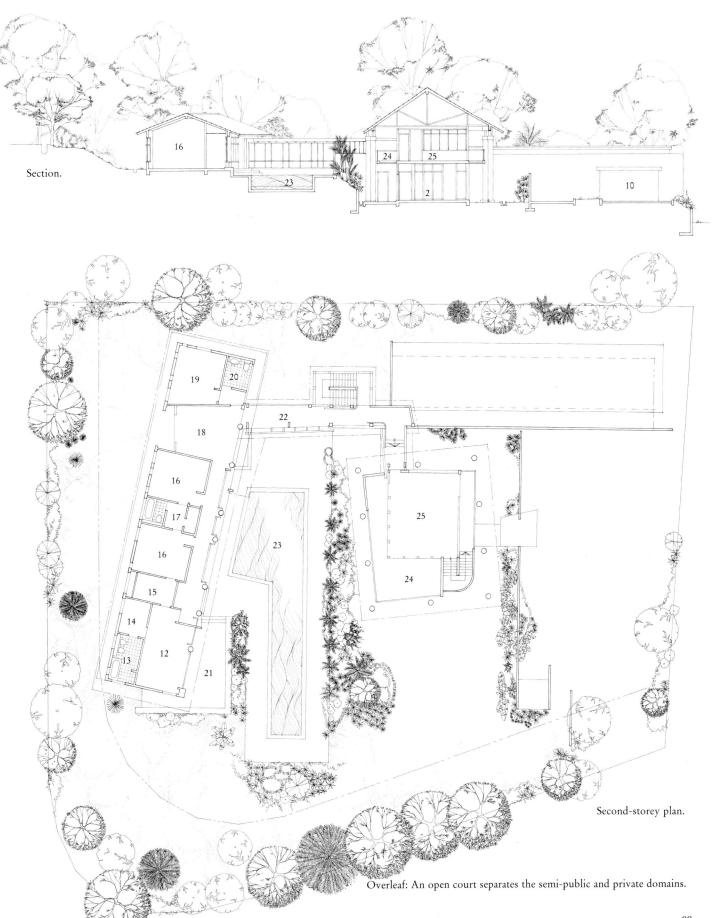

Section.

Second-storey plan.

Overleaf: An open court separates the semi-public and private domains.

99

corridor to the rear block, which is slightly rotated and is parallel with neither of the two geometries of the front block. This rear rectangle is a single-storey construction containing the private areas of the house: the bedrooms and family room, at a more intimate scale than the front block.

A subtle palette of colours is used throughout and the texture and grain of bricks, timber, floor tiles and slate emphasise the changes of function and geometry. The detailing reflects the broader intentions. Timber horizontal louvres and blinds filter sunlight; steel balustrades and column capitals have the contrast of modern and traditional materials that one sees in the work of the venetian architect Carlo Scarpa.

The house, for which the project architect was Lim Jin Geok, goes a long way towards successfully fusing a universal language of architecture with local/vernacular traditions and creating a regional modern architecture. It confirms the practice of William Lim Associates as one of the few in Asia making a serious contribution to this contemporary hybrid language.

The living room with the balcony beyond.

The bedrooms and the family area occupy a single-storey block.

The linkway connecting the two blocks.

THE GUNAWAN HOUSE

JAKARTA . JAVA
INDONESIA
ARCHITECT: TAN TJIANG AY, SOLICHIN GUNAWAN AND ANI ISDIATI
COMPLETED: 1991

The entrance porch or *serambi*.

Fond memories of boyhood days spent in a Dutch-designed plantation bunga-low in Central Java inspired Solichin Gunawan to build this house in a southern suburb of Jakarta. The fact that his wife Ani Isdiati has similar pleasant memories provided added motivation. They had lived for seven years in a rented property in Jakarta but with three young growing boys they decided to recreate their idyllic childhood days.

Gunawan is president of Atelier Enam Interiors, an independent offshoot of one of Indonesia's major architectural practices, and it may seem odd that he and his wife turned not to his highly respected architect colleagues, but to the small practice of Tan Tjiang Ay. Not so strange really, explains Gunawan: if he had entrusted the design to Atelier Enam, the house would have been done in an exemplary manner, but it would inevitably have taken secondary importance to the pressing needs of their clients.

Additionally, Ani Isdiati is a qualified architect who wished to be closely involved in the realisation of their house. Thus the final scheme is the result of a close collaboration between Ani Isdiati, who did the space programming, and architect Tan Tjiang Ay, who specialises in individual houses.

Gunawan is articulate about the precedence for the design – undeniably Dutch, he affirms; in the style of pre-war Dutch colonial bungalows in Indonesia. The selection of an appropriate site was done by Ani Isdiati.

The Gunawans describe their house as modest and simple. At 400 metre square floor area, it is not small but it has a basic simplicity and austerity in its form, language and materials. It is an exemplary solution for the tropics - it has a long, narrow plan form, mostly on one level, with natural cross ventilation assisted by ceiling fans. A wide verandah overlooks the garden. This is the principal circulation route and in addition is an outdoor living room.

The house is orientated roughly east to west. Thus the morning sun floods into the bedrooms. The verandah and sleeping areas are shaded from the heat of the afternoon sun.

Elsewhere the designers have incorporated conscious or sub-conscious references to traditional cultural patterns. The entrance porch overlooking the gateway has two wide built-in seats, memories of the *serambi*. This gives access to a reception room, formally arranged for guests who are not close family. The hierarchical arrangement of Asian houses is evident.

But the overpowering image conjured by the house is that of the planter's bungalow: a long, low roofline without gutters, and a terrace facing a garden. The double-height bedroom wing is counterbalanced in the composition by the water/generator tower.

The houses in this chapter are reinterpretations of traditional extended family compounds. Societies in Southeast Asia generally place great value on filial piety and it is common to find three or four generations of a family living together. It is the tradition of the extended family house raised on stilts along the Chao Phraya, or along the banks of the klongs in Bangkok, that provides the inspiration for the Niyom residence known as Bann Ton Son.

The Hadiprana family compound in Bali, set among the paddy fields of Tanah Gajah is similarly a reinterpretation of the traditional Balinese extended family house.

An intriguing aspect that enters the discourse is the notion of boundary. Boundaries in traditional compounds are ambiguous; often under-stood only by the inhabitants. The boundaries in a Malay kampong, or the Iban longhouse, are undetectable to a visitor from another culture. The reinterpretation of extended family dwellings into modern form could, by itself, form the subject of a book. Here, just two houses are identified as a segment of the spectrum of ideas expressed in contemporary Asian homes.

Bann Ton Son.

BANN TON SON

PLOENJIT ROAD
BANGKOK
THAILAND
ARCHITECT: PRAPAPAT AND THEERAPHON NIYOM . PLAN ARCHITECTS
COMPLETED: 1990

A pedestrian walkway gives access to the family compound.

Hidden from passers-by in a narrow lane off the Ploenjit Road, Bann Ton Son is an extended family compound of extraordinary beauty. Its impact is accentuated by the change of tempo when one steps from the narrow urban street alongside a *klong* into a garden of quiet tranquility.

Bangkok has a network of *klongs* penetrating most parts of the city. They still form a major transportation network, and are venues for markets. They were the original life-lines of Bangkok – indeed in former times Bangkok was a "water society". Many festivals were performed along the *klongs*, which have had an effect on Thai residential design.

Bann Ton Son has four separate dwellings within the family compound. The designers/owners, Prapapat and Theeraphon Niyom, both architects, live in one house with their two children. Adjacent and separated by a narrow external walkway is Prapapat Niyom's mother's house. The third house is occupied by her elder sister's family and the last house is the home of her brother's family.

The four houses are placed asymmetrically around a garden with connecting timber walkways, which pass over water-filled moats planted with hyacinth and water lily. At the heart of the compound is a pavilion and a shared family recreation pool. The walkways are reminiscent of the elevated timber pathways which served as entrances for houses alongside the Chao Phrya. Traditionally the walkways served a practical purpose of providing communications above the flood level of the river and bringing the people from their boats to their houses. Timber staircases would connect the walkway to the house.

One enters the compound through an outer yard, where the family's vehicles are accommodated. A narrow pedestrian walkway leads to the heart of the garden. The Niyom House is to the left of this alleyway.

The L-shaped plan contains three rooms at first storey: a family room, a large kitchen-dining room and a timber-floored verandah which looks out to the garden. This is the main entrance to the house, accessed by a short flight of steps from the timber walkway. This space is an interpretation of the traditional verandah facing the *klong*, where a family would sit to take advantage of the view. Maids' quarters and a utility area occupy a sub-basement which is cool and well-ventilated.

At second level, the main staircase leads to an elevated verandah outside the master bedroom. A further short flight of stairs leads to two children's bedrooms. The stair handrails are fashioned from oxen yokes recovered from a rural area.

The most significant aspect of the house is the assured way in which the architect handles the synthesis of modern technology reflective solar glazing,

The Niyom House is within the Bann Ton Son family compound.

The house is entered via a timber walkway.

Section.

The four family houses are placed asymmetrically around a garden.

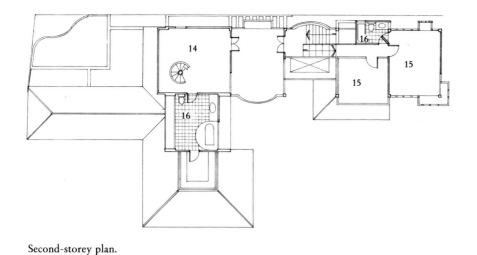

Second-storey plan.

1 maids' room
2 main storage
3 laundry
4 living
5 kitchen
6 dining
7 working and library
8 patio
9 pool
10 car park
11 court
12 lawn
13 guest room
14 master bedroom
15 bedroom
16 bathroom

0 1   5   10m

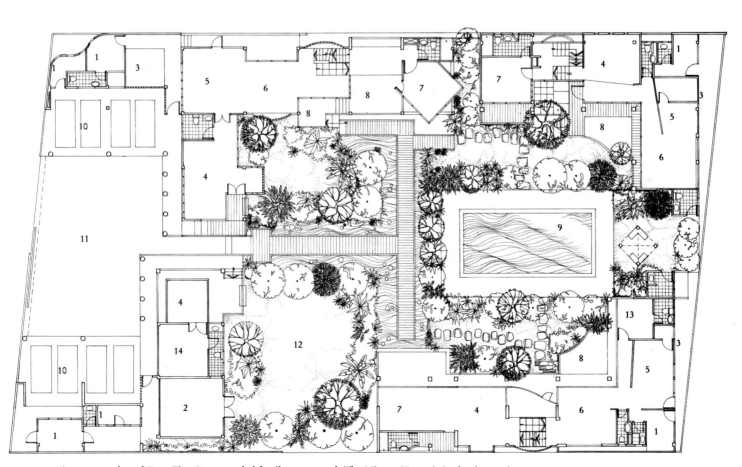

First-storey plan of Bann Ton Son extended family compound. The Niyom House is in the the southeast corner.
(The basement plan has been omitted for clarity. In the Niyom House it contains a music room and a guest room.)

air-conditioning and sliding aluminium glazing units – with traditional materials such as timber, stone and brick. Two architectural languages are fused without apparent difficulty.

There are innovations too: the louvred second-skin over the bathroom area (compare with Ken Yeang's Roof Roof House in Kuala Lumpur), and the water jets which automatically clean the outside surface of the all-glass bathroom. There is also an outdoor bathroom where the owner can shower under the open sky (compare with the Hadiprana House in Bali).

The first-storey floor finishes are grey-black granite, 'rooting' the house in the earth. Wall finishes are generally timber panels, which recall the materials of the traditional Thai house.

There is too the essence of a house in the tropics: a comfortable transition from inside to outside. The naturally ventilated verandahs and lobbies optimise on breezes and turbulent air currents. The relationship between the moats, timber bridges, walkways and elevated house entrances all relate to traditional patterns. The memories of traditional housing are overpowering.

The entrance is deliberately kept modest and low key but is constantly guarded. Roofs do not have gutters. Water is shed onto the ground and thence into the linear moats, which demarcate individual house boundaries and act as barriers and channels of circulation. The landscaping is sensitively conceived and perfectly compliments the architectural language. The house has other links with tradition, including the use of fish-scale tiles and horizontal timber cladding, used extensively on the house facade.

This house affirms Prapapat and Theeraphon Niyom as major figures in the contemporary architecture of Southeast Asia. The Niyoms are examples of a confident new generation of Thai architects.

The roof over the Niyom House is partially louvred.

Open-to-sky bathroom.

Dining area with garden beyond.

Stair hall between the master bedroom and children's bedrooms.

THE HADIPRANA HOUSE

TANAH GAJAH, BALI
INDONESIA
ARCHITECTS : HENDRA HADIPRANA AND FARIED
MASDOEKI . GRAHACIPTA HADIPRANA
COMPLETED : 1989

The *angkul* (entrance gate).

The family complex of the Hadiprana family is situated at Tanah Gajah, a rural area of Bali, east of Ubud. Hendra Hadiprana acquired the site in 1980 and commenced building two years later. The concept, developed with the assistance of architect Faried Masdoeki, is that of an extended family compound, with individual dwellings for his family of two married daughters and a married son. Other pavilions are being added for guests. There is, in addition, a central *balegede* (family pavilion), a dining pavilion, a library pavilion, a fitness pavilion and a swimming pool.

On slightly elevated ground, to the southern edge of the compound is *Pondok Margin*, the house of the head of the family. It stands slightly apart from the other dwellings, separated by a gentle cascade of rice terraces. As befits its status, it is the only house in the group to have a double *meru* roof. The family hall has this distinction too – all other buildings have simple pitched roof. The distancing and height of *Pondok Margin* is symbolic of the position of family head and it is a rare privilege for a visitor to penetrate, up to this extent, into the family hierarchy.

The whole complex is on an east-facing slope. The visitor crosses a narrow private bridge over a river valley and halts at the foot of a flight of stone stairs leading to the *angkul* (entrance gate). Ascending through the gateway, the path inclines to the left and then aligns on an east-west axis astride which sits the symmetrical main hall at the heart of the complex.

The house of the 'head' of the family is approached by a slightly circuitous route along the contours of the hillside, passing alongside the reflective waters of the rice paddy. The path offers a sequence of changing views of the house, before finally approaching from the west. This suspends the enjoyment of the private living room and the *pendopo* at the Eastern end of the house.

One enters through the south facing entrance portico into a narrow hallway running from east to west. To the right is the living area with verandah doors opening to a north-facing panorama. More doors in the east facade give access to a spacious, free standing *pendopo* – open on all sides and raised on a stone podium. Opening off the living room is a kitchen and a breakfast room facing south over neighbouring paddy fields. At the opposite end of the entrance hall is the master bedroom, the bathroom and the dressing room.

The roof is carried on a grid of circular timber columns, fashioned from trunks of coconut palm trees. These support beams of *bingkrai* (close in appearance to teak). Facing bricks are used throughout and have been painted white. The floor surfaces are of terracotta tiles and concrete, with an exposed aggregate finish. Wall finishes and furniture are in a subtle range of green and white. The

Above: The main house is a slight distance from the other dwellings.
Overleaf: *Pondok Margin* is sited on slightly elevated ground.

The *pendopo* alongside the main house.

Below the living room terrace is a fish pond.

Section.

A bridge connecting the two pavilions.

1 entrance porch
2 *lanai*
3 living room/music room
4 dining area
5 corridor
6 storage
7 toilet
8 pantry
9 bridge
10 hall
11 study
12 master bedroom
13 bathroom
14 walk-in closet
15 pool
16 pool terrace
17 bedroom
18 guest room
19 maids' room
20 kitchen
21 service area
22 driver's room
23 garage
24 staff toilets

0 1   5   10m

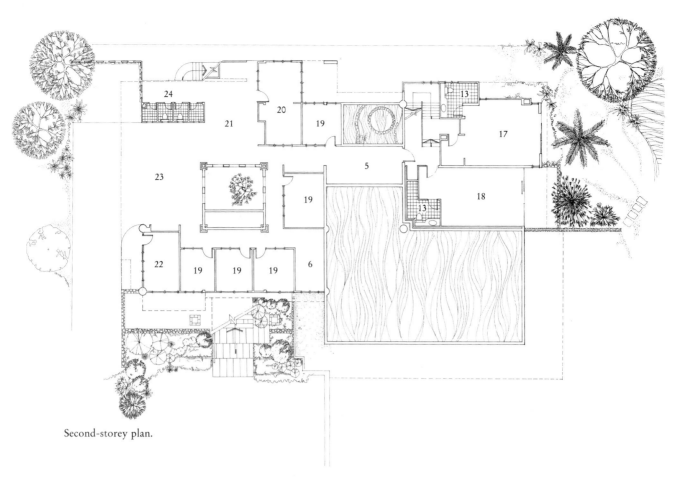

Second-storey plan.

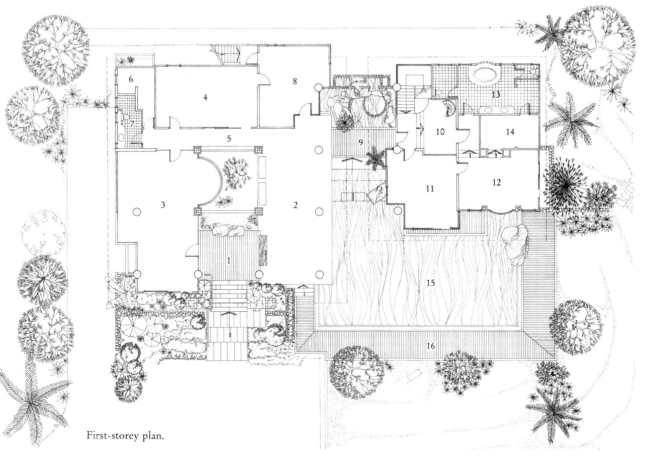

First-storey plan.

131

BANN RIM NAM

SOMPONG-PETCHAREE
BANGKOK
THAILAND
ARCHITECT: NITHI STHAPITANONDA . ARCHITECTS 49
COMPLETED: 1990

The house with the Chao Phraya River
in the background.

The Sompong-Petcharee house is one of a group within a family compound known as Bann Rim Nam. It has a unique location on the bank of the Chao Phraya river with an impressive new suspension bridge in the background. The Thai owner is of Chinese ethnic origins.

The house has a slightly austere appearance with white-painted concrete structure and metallic grey roofing tiles. A distinctly 'Oriental' feel pervades, due to a series of low-pitched roofs which step down from a two-storey element in the centre, to a riverside terrace and an entrance porch.

There is a firm, controlled relationship of elements and materials. The house form suggests solid strength; it has a rather heavy structure, and the terrace roof is firmly supported on circular concrete columns.

The solidity of the form is lightened by the tripartite arrangement of the elevations. The first storey is expressed as a podium with raised parapet wall, the upper (second) storey is recessed behind this parapet and the roofs project beyond the upper floors. This accentuates the horizontality and the 'rootedness' of the dwelling.

In plan, the house is a 'U' shape enclosing a courtyard with a lily pond and a fountain. Planting is formally arranged and tightly controlled. Concrete walkways over the pool reinterpret the timber walkways found in the traditional Thai riverside house.

In scale and formality the house is slightly smaller and less monumental in appearance than the neighbouring *Uthane-Suwanna* house, the residence of the patriarch of the family.

This house reflects an affluent and exclusive lifestyle, a retreat from the frenetic city life of Bangkok. In this dwelling, Nithi Sthapitanonda continues his search for an appropriate expression for the contemporary Thai house.

The 'U' shaped plan encloses a lily pond.

The house has a series of low-pitched roofs.

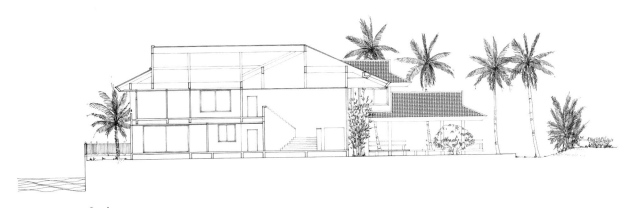

Section.

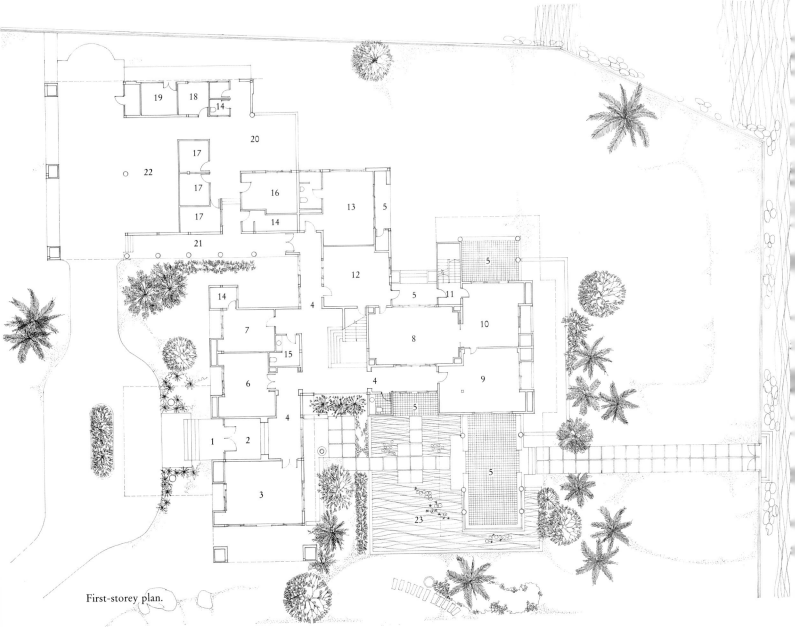

First-storey plan.

The courtyard viewed from the stairwell.

Second-storey plan.

0 1   5   10m

1 entrance porch
2 lobby
3 living room
4 corridor
5 terrace
6 study
7 barber
8 banquet room
9 sitting room
10 dining room
11 hall
12 pantry
13 guest room
14 store
15 toilet
16 kitchen
17 maids' room
18 driver's room
19 mechanics room
20 laundry
21 covered walkway
22 garage
23 lily pond
24 Chao Phraya River
25 corridor
26 private living room
27 bedroom
28 pantry
29 walk-in closet
30 prayer room
31 bathroom
32 bedroom
33 sitting room
34 balcony
35 hall

THE LO HOUSE

JALAN LOKUS . LUYAND
KOTA KINABALU . SABAH
EAST MALAYSIA
ARCHITECT: WONG KAH HO . WAY ARCHITECTS
COMPLETED: 1980

The roof dominates the house and provides sun-shading to windows.

The Lo House, built for the Kota Kinabalu representative of the Standard Chartered Bank, was one of architect Wong Kah Ho's first commissions when he returned to Sabah after receiving his education in the UK and having worked some years in London, Bahrain and Saudi Arabia.

The house contains much of the intensity and single-mindedness of a fledgling practice. If it exhibits a little naïveté and lack of resolution in detailed junctions, it nevertheless is a powerful exploration of the principles of the Modern Movement translated into a tropical context.

The *parti* for the house is the Borneo longhouse. Traditionally, such a house built in a narrow linear form had a central aisle or corridor. Different family spaces and functions were disposed on either side of this axis. The narrow plan form permitted maximum cross ventilation and the longhouse would be sited to take advantage of aspect, contours, breezes and other climatic constraints. The Lo House is entirely air-conditioned, but when windows on both of the long sides are opened, it is not uncomfortable without air-conditioning.

In a house for an ethnic Chinese banker, this analogy with the Iban longhouse can only be taken so far. The architect does not volunteer the information – the analogy is introduced in a way which suggests that it is more a sub-conscious than a conscious factor in the design.

Perhaps the same is true of the *feng-shui* of the house. The house sits on a slope which faces southeast and overlooks the distant views of the South China Sea. To the northwest is a hill, to the southwest, a defile which the access road follows. Whether this siting is a conscious decision is unclear, but the orientation of the house is a conscious act; in this manner, the windows, shaded by a heavy roof overhang, avoid the path of the sun, which moves almost directly overhead in these latitudes. This is one of the clearest indications that the architect understands the necessity to adapt the planar surfaces of the Modern Movement aesthetic and to create a dark horizontal roofline, which cuts the air-

Section.

The house with Mount Kinabalu in the background.

Elevation.

conditioning load by substantially cooling the walls of the principal rooms. There is a synthesis of modernist form with the vernacular form.

There is in the house an underlying `Asian' hierarchy. The grand double-storey high entrance portico, with its collection of ancient cannons, leads to a reception hall. The hall is arranged with a screen wall which masks off the family living areas. This is the arrangement one finds in a traditional Chinese house, and it is complemented by the client's selection of antique furniture. The family is Christian, therefore there is no family altar here. Nevertheless, the arrangement conveys a memory and cultural continuity. Beyond the lobby is the main family room, which opens out onto a verandah looking south towards Mount Kinabalu, Asia's highest peak.

To the right, on entering are the dining areas, a breakfast room and a Western-style kitchen, and beyond, an open-to-sky Asian cooking area and staff accommodation. To the left, the long corridor leads to a bedroom wing. At second storey is the master bedroom, a private family room and a study.

The roof appears from a distance to be of concrete construction. This appearance is deceptive, it is in fact made of asbestos-cement sheet, and its heavy appearance is mitigated by the length of the house.

The form of the house is a response to a specific client and site conditions, but the Lo House has generating principles which are worthy of further study in our efforts to fuse modernist ideas within the tropical regional context.

The double-storey high entrance portico.

The linear plan form has a central corridor.

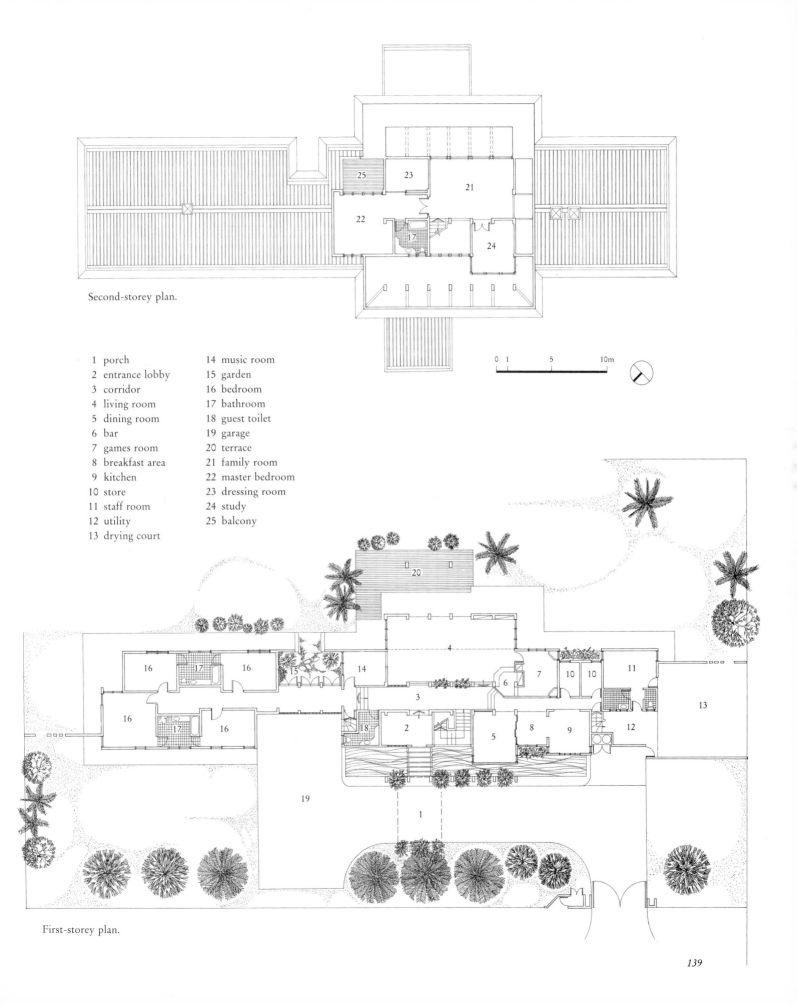

Second-storey plan.

1 porch
2 entrance lobby
3 corridor
4 living room
5 dining room
6 bar
7 games room
8 breakfast area
9 kitchen
10 store
11 staff room
12 utility
13 drying court
14 music room
15 garden
16 bedroom
17 bathroom
18 guest toilet
19 garage
20 terrace
21 family room
22 master bedroom
23 dressing room
24 study
25 balcony

0 1   5   10m

First-storey plan.

THE RAZAK HARRIS HOUSE

KOTA KINABALU . SABAH
EAST MALAYSIA
ARCHITECT: WONG KAH HO . WAY ARCHITECTS
COMPLETED: 1989

The courtyard between the formal living room and the reception/games room, with covered link.

This house marks a further step in the search for a modern tropical architecture for East Malaysia. Wong Kah Ho expresses unashamed admiration for Tengku Adlin's House (page 152). It should, he feels, have signalled a direction for modern architecture in Sabah when it was designed in the late 1970's, instead, in the following decade few houses of real architectural quality emerged.

In the plan form of the Razak Harris House the principal rooms have a north aspect whilst on the short east and west elevations the architect has created deeply recessed facades with sun-filtering devices. At midday when the sun is almost directly overhead, sunlight is allowed to enter vertically into a two-storey high light well between the dining and living rooms. The effect is stunning in an otherwise dim interior – the light moves poetically across this space around noon, reflecting upon louvred concrete walls and highlighting two etched glass screens on either side of the light well. It is the focus of the house and reminds one of Louis Kahn's maxim that light is the giver of form.

One can be critical of the house's almost complete reliance on air-conditioning. Although it is possible to open the windows in the living room to give cross ventilation, this is rarely done by the owner.

The house is designed as two blocks connected by a corridor. The entrance is at approximately the midpoint of the longer block on the south elevation and leads to an entrance lobby. The lobby leads in turn to the tall light well, with, to the right, the dining room, and to the left, the informal living room. At a lower level is the formal living room. Across a small courtyard beyond the formal area, via a covered walkway, is a reception/games room.

The courtyard and the reception room can be accessed directly from the main driveway, which means that receptions can be held by the owner, without guests having to enter the private areas of his dwelling.

Thus within a modern form and architectural expression the architect has integrated traditional cultural practices. The kitchen is relegated to the extreme east end of the plan, again reflecting traditional practice in which the *rumah dapur* is at the rear of the house. On the upper level of the house is a family room and four bedrooms, including the master bedroom suite.

The aesthetic is unquestionably modern, the interplay of cubic volumes and light attests to the architect's clear distancing of himself from the vernacular model and a belief that a modern state requires a modern architecture. Both the owner and the architect are to be applauded for a clear indication of a direction for a modern Sabah architecture, which nevertheless has integrated some elements of traditional cultural practices and climatic responses.

White planar surfaces give a modernist aesthetic.

The entrance driveway.

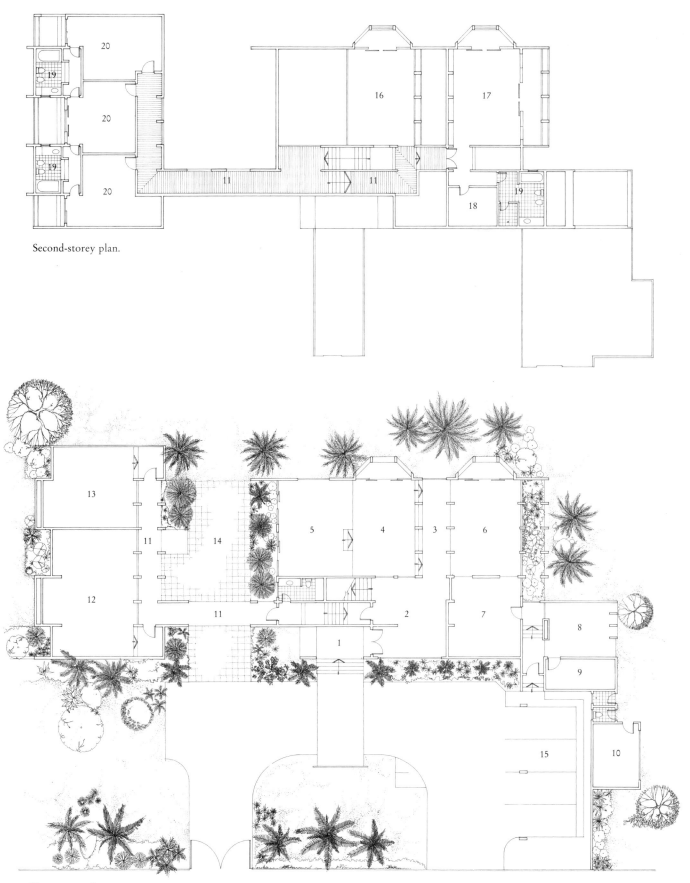

Second-storey plan.

First-storey plan.

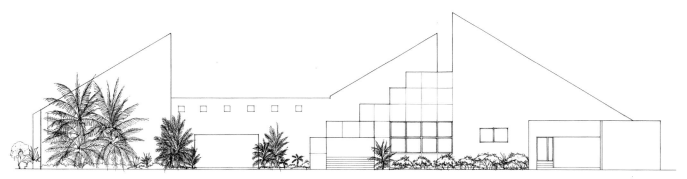

Elevation.

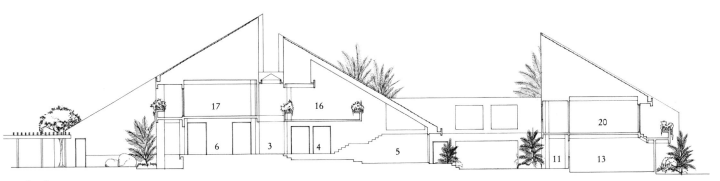

Section.

1 porch
2 entrance/gallery
3 hallway
4 informal living
5 formal living
6 dining room
7 main kitchen/breakfast room
8 service kitchen
9 pantry/laundry
10 staff room

11 corridor
12 entertainment/games room
13 storage
14 courtyard
15 garage
16 family room
17 master bedroom
18 dressing room
19 bathroom
20 bedroom

The dramatic two-storey high lightwell between the dining and living rooms.

Sun filtering devices to bedroom windows on the west elevation.

The entrance/gallery with central lightwell beyond.

THE VACHARPHOL HOUSE

SUKHOTHAI ROAD
BANGKOK
THAILAND
ARCHITECT: JOHN RIFENBERG . RIFENBERG ASSOCIATES, ARCHITECTS
COMPLETED: 1990

The living room terrace.

Featured as Thailand's "house of the year" in the 1991 edition of *Bann Nai Fun*, this is an elegant residence. It is the work of the Rifenberg Associates (formerly Rifenberg/Rirkrit) practice, which was established in 1964 and has built up a considerable reputation as designers of refined houses.

Situated on a site off Sukhothai Road, and the home of a prominent businesswoman in Bangkok, it is a house of exquisite proportions, based on a plan revolving around a central double-height stairwell.

There is a Thai essence to the house, although it does not draw directly upon traditional models. The elevation has a tripartite arrangement. The heavy base is 'rooted' in the earth, with deeply recessed windows. It has a precise, angular, modernist language, and is finished in white, glazed tiles. The language is in a direct line from Corbusier, Marcel Breuer and in the precision of late modernists such as Richard Meier. The second storey is lighter with a double skin: external glass and internal opaque rice paper screens; almost Japanese in appearance. In the bedrooms, this opaque inner skin is replaced by white-painted, horizontal louvred screens giving greater privacy. The third element, the roof, floats above this lighter element, supported on sturdy circular columns. It is an elegant solution which reduces the scale of the facades.

The essence of Thai traditional architecture is most vividly portrayed in the extensive use of timber-panelled walls, doors and ceilings, internally, and in the timber-latticed screens. It is also expressed in the delicately inlaid, timber parquet floors.

At the heart of the house is a high, internal, glazed atrium, bringing natural light into the stairwell and indoor rock garden. The walls of this inner hall are teak-panelled, surfacing memories of traditional domestic interiors.

The architectural language of the house is undeniably that of the Modern Movement. The modern influence is however cleverly synthesised with Thai timber craftsmanship and the pitched-roof element, to create a regional modern architecture which goes some way to answering Paul Ricoeur's rhetorical question "How to become modern and to maintain roots in one's cultural past?"[1]

[1] Ricoeur, Paul, "Universal Civilisation and National Cultures" in History and Truth, Evanston, 1966.

The swimming pool court at night.

The dining room.

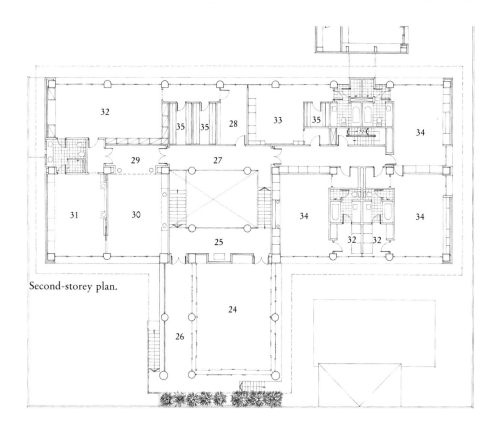

Second-storey plan.

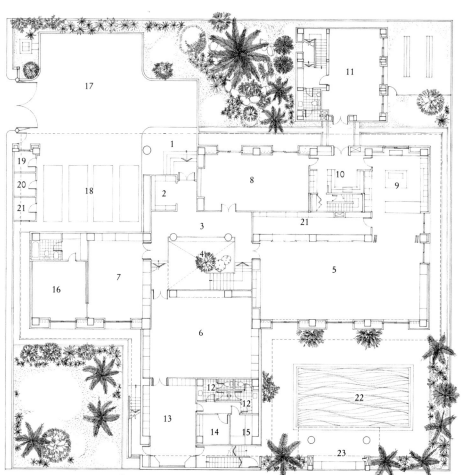

First-storey plan.

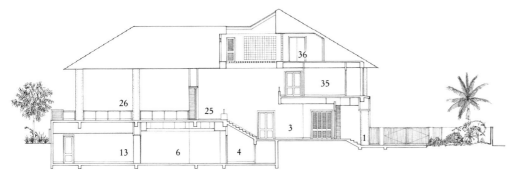

Section/Elevation.

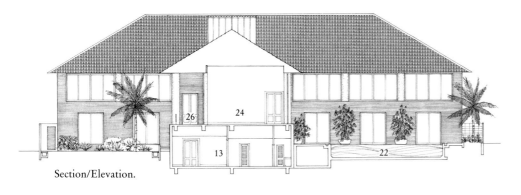

Section.

1 entrance
2 shoes room
3 entrance hall
4 lower court
5 family room
6 music room
7 library
8 dining room
9 kitchen
10 pantry
11 Thai kitchen
12 bathroom
13 exercise room
14 massage
15 sauna
16 guest bedroom
17 motor court
18 garage
19 security guard

20 mechanical equipment room
21 storage
22 swimming pool
23 swimming pool bar
24 living room
25 landing
26 terrace
27 upper landing
28 Buddha room
29 foyer
30 sitting room
31 bedroom
32 dressing room
33 nursery/bedroom
34 bedroom
35 walk-in closet
36 work room
37 laundry
38 electric meters

0 1   5   10m

The entrance with the entrance hall beyond.

The living room.

The library adjoining the guest bedroom.

The central stairwell with dramatic daylighting from above.

TENGKU ADLIN HOUSE

KOTA KINABALU . SABAH
EAST MALAYSIA
ARCHITECT: LEE SENG LOONG . LEESENGLOONG ARCHITECTS
COMPLETED: 1978

A modest entrance softened by landscaping.

The residence of Tengku Zainal Adlin in Sabah overlooks the Straits of Kota Kinabalu harbour. Designed in the late 1970's, it still retains its pristine modernist qualities, now softened by the bougainvillea and flowering fruit trees that have grown to maturity around the house.

The owner is the indefatigable Deputy Director of the Sabah Foundation (*Yayasan Sabah*), whose interests extend far beyond the socio-economic advancement of Malaysians into every aspect of life. He is intensely active in the conservation of wildlife. Indeed one of the largest flowers in the world, the *Rafflesia tengku adlinii*, is named after this prince of the Malay nobility.

Despite his respect for tradition and heritage, Tengku Adlin's house is the epitome of the modernist aesthetic. The white concrete box is carried on four square, concrete columns, soaring above the precipitous site.

The main pedestrian entrance is across a timber footbridge, which penetrates a square, concrete tube emerging into the double-height volume of the living area. Four bedrooms on the upper floor look down into this central space. Beneath the living room and accessible externally is a family room.

Below the house are thickly wooded slopes which, though they have suffered from 'flash' fires that plague the forest in dry months, present a thick forest canopy just below the living room terrace. The natural habitat has been supplemented by flowering ornamental varieties.

The house is located on the ridge of Signal Hill, and has a panoramic view of Gaya Island and the South China Sea beyond. A mirrored wall in the living room reflects the rays of the setting sun into the dining area. Silver mirror glass is used extensively throughout the house. It reduces the radiant heat load from the western sun and blends with the white planar surfaces.

The striking feature of the house is its coolness, even on the hottest days. This coolness is achieved by an ingenious system of updrafts. Beneath the house, alongside the entrance bridge is a substantial void. At the rear of the living room is a timber-louvred air well, so that air rises up the hillside and blows directly into the living room from below. When the terrace doors are opened, or the master bedroom shutters drawn back, this cooling breeze reaches all parts of the house.

Hot air rises through the central void and is channelled and released through an air gap at the highest point of the glazed skylight. This is an example of the natural ventilation techniques of the kampong hut, reinterpreted into modern architectural language. Above the double-height living area is a glass-louvred roof, which filters the sun and creates a complex pattern of light on the timber-panelled walls.

The house viewed from the entrance gate.

The house overlooks the South China Sea.

The panoramic view from the terrace.

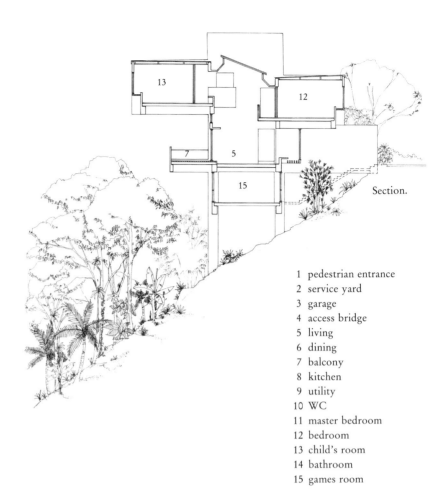

Section.

1 pedestrian entrance
2 service yard
3 garage
4 access bridge
5 living
6 dining
7 balcony
8 kitchen
9 utility
10 WC
11 master bedroom
12 bedroom
13 child's room
14 bathroom
15 games room

The air-well below the living room.

Living and dining areas evoke memories of the traditional kampong hut's spatial demarcation. Areas are defined by slight variations in floor level. A single step up to the dining space, a step down to a family sitting area.

The house is a lucid statement of the principles of the Modern Movement, modified by climatic and cultural responses. It is seminal and should, if it had been more widely appreciated, have given a signal for the direction of modern Sabah architecture in the 1980's.

The Tengku Zainal Adlin house is the result of a collaboration of an owner, who has thought deeply about his relationship to the modernisation process within his own culture, and an inspired work by a relatively unheralded Singapore-based architect. The house refocuses the direction of architecture in East Malaysia.

The double-height living area.

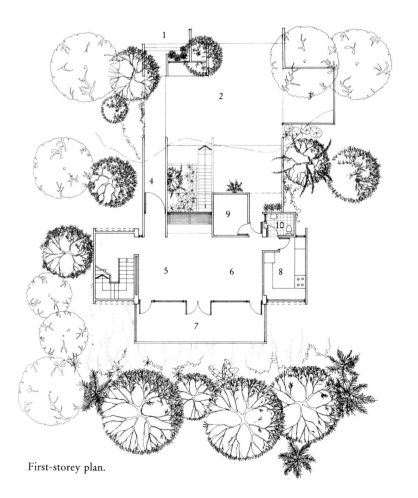

First-storey plan.

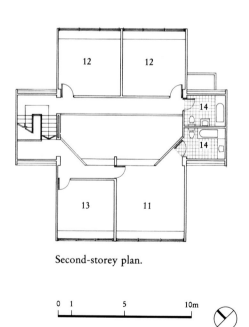

Second-storey plan.

0 1   5   10m

155

THE ZULUETA HOUSE

TAGATAY CITY
PHILIPPINES
DESIGNER: BUDJI LAYUG
COMPLETED: 1984

The house sits on a mountain ridge.

For Budji Layug, the Zulueta House was one of his first major design commissions, although he is internationally respected for his furniture designs in rattan, leather, rope and *Mactan* stone, which are much sought after in Los Angeles, New York and Manila.

The house was a labour of love, resulting from a collaboration with the owner who, sadly, lived in it for only three years before he died. Budji Layug reveals little of their working relationship, but it is evident that he was given considerable freedom to choose materials, finishes and items of furniture, and that the design was the result of close empathy with the client's lifestyle and taste, allied to his own considerable design talents.

In the course of the construction of the house, Budji Layug and the owner spontaneously adjusted walls, moulded the interior, responded to views from the site, and simply allowed the house to grow from the land. The swirling, organic form appears to emulate the rice terrace on the mountain slopes of Banaue, a curving sensuous form that grows out of the hillside. The retaining walls of quarried, angular stones, that extend outwards from the house create terraces, and bind the house to its location. The entrance gate, made of steel and distressed native canoes, is set in a fortress-like rock wall.

The house sits almost at the crest of a mountain ridge. From the stepped living room of the house, with its several platforms, large, glazed windows look to the horizon and a distant volcano in a lake. On occasions, the view from the window is of banks of clouds obscuring the valley below.

The death of the owner has sadly led to the deterioration of the exterior, but this does not obscure the integrity of the design; indeed, it gives it a patina, as though the land is embracing and claiming the house as its own.

Descending the stairs from the entrance lobby, with their natural timber handrails, one is reminded of the interiors of Antonio Gaudi in Barcelona, or the plasticity of Eero Saarinen's work. The interior walls are rendered in white limestone plaster, with sea shells revealed on the surface.

Throughout, the floor, like that of the Locsin House, is of granite blocks originally brought to the Philippines as ships ballast in early trading vessels from China. The stairs and level changes are created using granite, so that the exterior terraces are carried through into the interior, following the contour lines of the mountain; a morphological memory stamped indelibly on the house form.

Aluminium frames to the main windows are incongruous, and the designer admits that, but for the remoteness of the site, he would have used glass without frames. Above the main living space is a circular rooflight, which permits a shaft of sunlight to orchestrate patterns on the floor and walls and to act as a sundial.

Most of the furniture is of Budji Layug's own design: rock tables, leather-upholstered chairs and rattan lounge chairs. The emphasis is on nature and natural materials: timber, granite, rock, pebbles, and volcanic ash, which is used as a roof covering.

Above the dining table is a 'primitive' work of art, a wall hanging from the Igorot tribe incorporating shells, fibres, reeds and coconut husks. The floor in the dining area changes to *narra* timber, and low walls alongside the staircase reflect the natural landforms. The living space is dominated by a giant, three-metre-high piece of driftwood on a granite base. Many of Layug's furniture creations are in bamboo, a humble material which he has raised to the status of a designer material, thus signalling new directions in Philippine furniture design.

The house is totally at one with its site, as though hewn from the mountain, rooted in the land yet soaring towards the sky, strong yet sensual; the work of an artist who is in love with the land and who has an intimate understanding of local materials.

The entrance gate.

The roof terrace overlooks an inland lake and volcanic island.

Plastered walls reflect the natural landforms.

Above: The master bedroom and dressing room.
Left: Panoramic views from the living area.

A curved staircase descends
to the living area.

1 living area
2 dining area
3 kitchen
4 service kitchen
5 master bedroom
6 jacuzzi
7 dressing room
8 bedroom
9 toilet and bathroom
10 staff bedroom
11 staff living room
12 staff kitchen/dining
13 store
14 staff toilet and bathroom
15 pool
16 *lanai*
17 sauna room beneath terrace
18 rooflight
19 roof terrace
20 entrance lobby
21 garage
22 entrance driveway

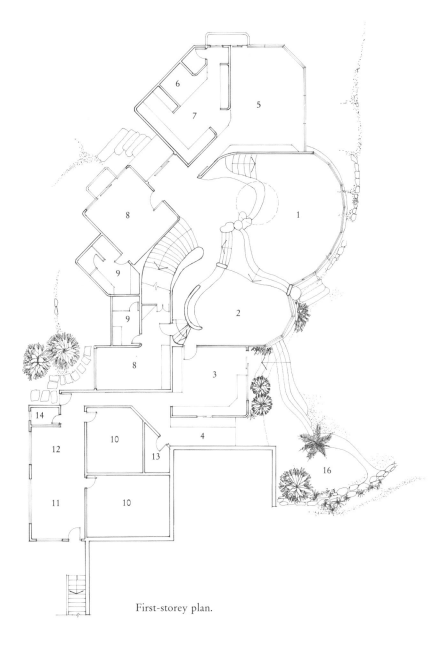

First-storey plan.

0 1   5   10m

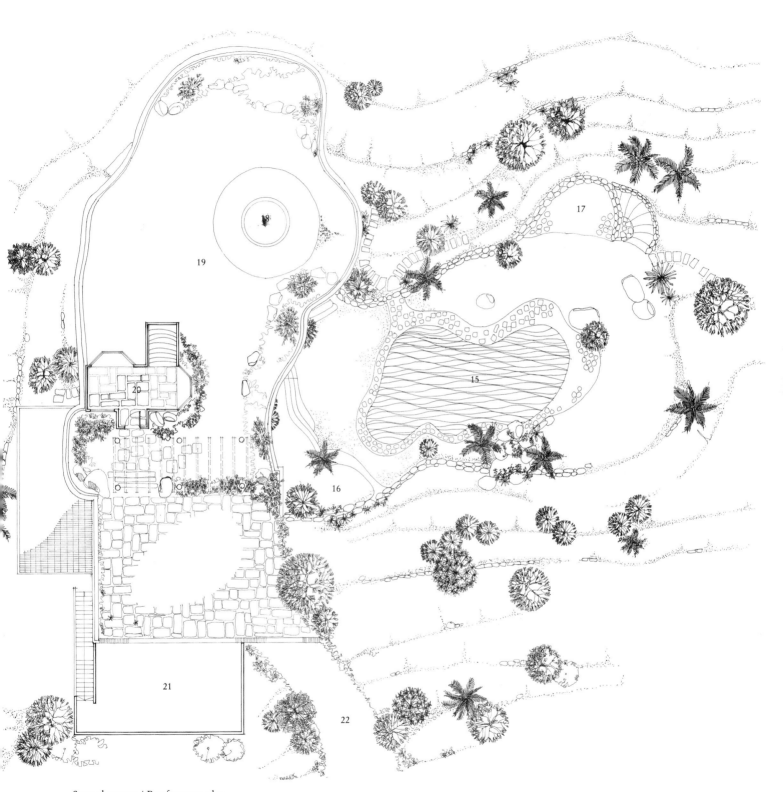

Second-storey / Roof terrace plan.

THE ROOF ROOF HOUSE

SELANGOR
MALAYSIA
ARCHITECT: KEN YEANG . TR HAMZAH AND YEANG
COMPLETED: 1984

Patterns of light and shade created by the louvred roof.

The Roof Roof House is the most widely known of Ken Yeang's buildings. The house is a serious attempt to test his theoretical ideas of architecture as a climatic filter. The form is undeniably Modernist and in the language of Le Corbusier. The architect's ideas on sun shading, a double-roof, and the development of his propositions on 'filter' architecture, are examined. Yeang sees building enclosures as environmental filters and interprets this idea into built form. The outer curved roof acts as a solar filter to the rest of the house, and the moveable, internal glass partitions and panels, theoretically, are the adjustable parts that can be manipulated to control the wind-flow and thus the internal micro-climate.

The first storey consists of a living room that looks out to a shaded swimming pool. Yeang sees the pool area as an extension of the living area. Circular stairs lead from the living room to the upper gallery, while a short flight of steps leads down to the dining area.

A curved, waist-high wall separates the living and dining areas. From the dining room, there is access to the kitchen whilst another door leads to the entrance hall – an open passage with security grills at either end, which permit cross ventilation.

The second storey consists of a gallery, a family space, the master bedroom suite and two smaller rooms. The family hall is connected to the ground floor by an air well, and thence to the roof by a roof ventilator.

A glass door opens from the family hall onto a terrace that is the roof of the car-porch. Off the hall are stairs that give access to the roof terrace, which is kept cool by the sweeping filter pergola over the entire house.

The house is not without faults, and some of the 'valve' devices that Ken Yeang incorporates require considerable effort to balance. The design principle is that the prevailing winds blow over the pool into the living room and, by adjusting the openings in the sliding patio doors and another opening in the side elevation of the building, comfortable conditions will be achieved.

The Roof Roof House confirms Ken Yeang as an architect of serious intention, possessing wit and sensitivity; an architect with an intellectual rigour behind his work.

There is poetry in the building. It is technically fascinating, and the play of light, as the sun moves across the louvred roof and the walls, is truly delightful. It looks magical in the morning sunlight. The effect of the juxtaposition of one element over another is breathtaking; the clarity of edges, shadow lines and dark recesses – all the elements that make modern architecture so stimulating, are present. It is a seminal building in modern tropical architecture.

Above: The house viewed from the northeast corner of the garden.
Overleaf: The outer curved roof acts as a solar filter.

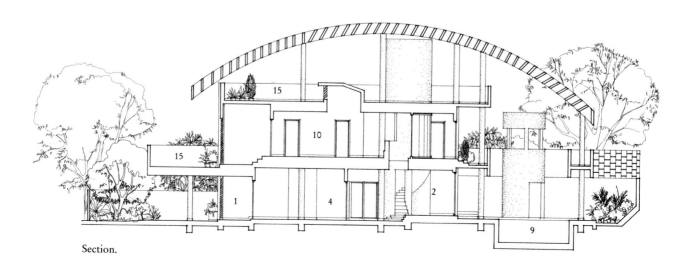

Section.

1 shoe lobby
2 living
3 dining
4 play
5 guest room
6 kitchen
7 laundry
8 maid
9 pool
10 lounge
11 bedroom
12 sleeping
13 gallery
14 bathroom
15 roof terrace
16 carport

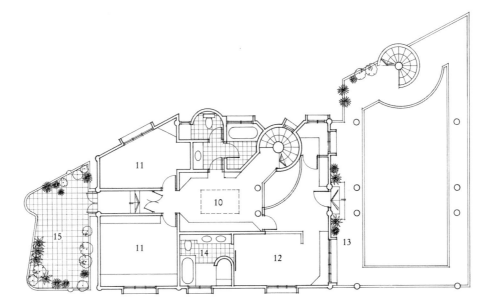

Second-storey plan.

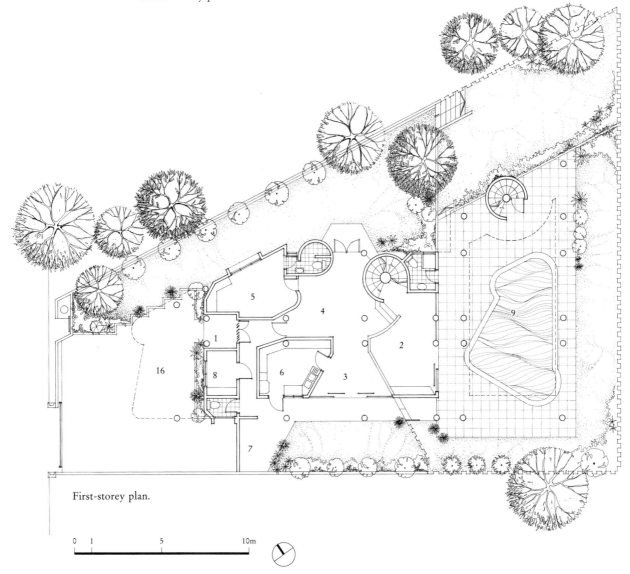

First-storey plan.

0   1   5   10m

THE MOUNTBATTEN ROAD HOUSE

SINGAPORE
ARCHITECT: TANG GUAN BEE
COMPLETED: 1988

The living space is a triple-height volume.

The architecture of Tang Guan Bee evokes extremes of critical acclaim and dislike. Those of the former persuasion point to his masterly compositional skills, artistic preoccupation with colour, and interplay of planes and volumes. Others are critical of these qualities, pronouncing them brash and abrasive. Tang is unfazed by the criticism and he has corporate and individual clients, who find his colourful and controversial compositions to their liking.

There are similarities in this house, which is one of a pair, with the fragmented qualities of Frank Gehry's Norton House on Venice Beach in Los Angeles. It does not, however, have the sense of impermanence that Gehry conveys with his use of industrial materials, such as wire mesh and rough timber.

Beneath the outward display of exuberance is a serious concern for tropical living and for cultural continuity. Tang says that, "there are four separate units in the house – the guesthouse at the front, the pool, the family house and then the servant's quarters. The concept is much like the old Chinese houses, where you have an outer guesthouse and then the inner house, where the host lives".[1]

In this and other works, the architect combines a firm control of structure, with a collage of forms, materials and colour. Yet his designs never descend into 'kitsch' or chaos; the complexity, the clashing of angles, the juxtaposition of materials retains an overall coherence.

Tang has happily compromised particular details to meet the requirements of the client's *feng-shui* advisor. A window to the living room has been slightly angled, the gibbet-like projections on the carpark roof structure have been cut off. These modifications do not, however, seriously detract from the overall appearance, as they might on a more symmetrical facade. And the architect acknowledges that the client's own modifications to the perimeter fence have improved upon the original. The house, in other words, is not static, it can change, grow and fit the mood of the client.

The entrance hall opens off a barrel-vaulted carport. To the side of the entrance there is a reception room, and at second storey, a guest bedroom lit by clerestory in a raised square tower, which is rotated in relation to the main geometry of the house.

An elevated gallery leads to the family living area. The gallery has a curved polycarbonate roof and glass-block floor. The swimming pool slips beneath this gallery, and there is deliberate ambiguity between the inside and the outside of the dwelling.

The largest element in the composition, at the rear of the site, is covered by

---

[1] Thio Lay Hoon. *House of Controversy* Interior Digest.

Above: The house conveys informality, friendliness and an individual personality.
Right: The family area and the steps up to the elevated gallery beyond.

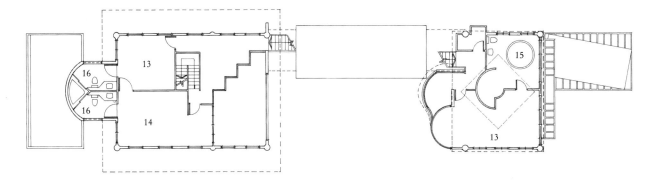

Second-storey plan.

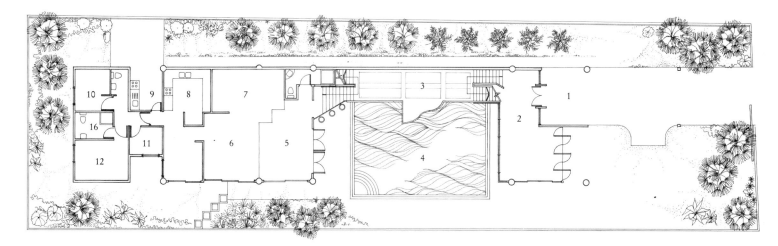

First-storey plan.

0 1   5   10m

The skylight above the guest suite lights the walk-in closet.

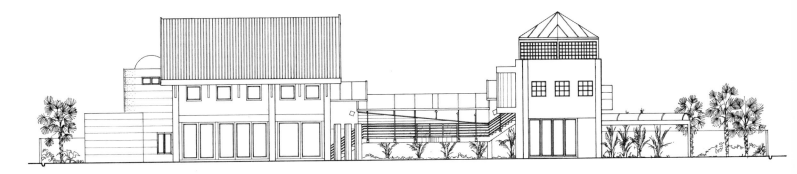

Elevation.

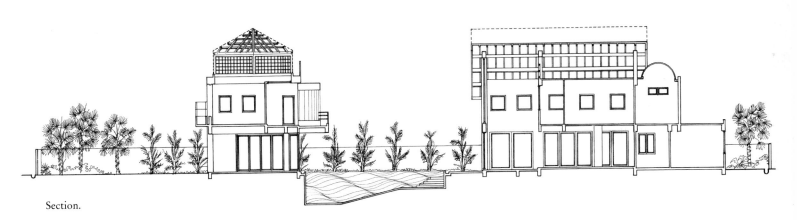

Section.

Front elevation.

1 carport
2 hall/reception
3 gallery
4 swimming pool
5 lounge
6 dining
7 living
8 kitchen
9 outdoor kitchen
10 utility
11 storage
12 maid
13 bedroom
14 master bedroom
15 jacuzzi
16 bathroom
(Not shown: family area at mezzanine level)

In Singapore the convention is to refer
to the ground floor as the first-storey.
The upper floor of a two-storey house is
thus referred to as the second-storey.
I have tried to keep to this convention
throughout.

All the plans have been redrawn and
they are accurate. With regard to the
landscape I have relied in most cases
upon photographs and site notes. There
may therefore be inaccuracies in the
exact position or in some cases the
variety of tree depicted; but the relationship to the built form is close to reality.

- Robert Powell

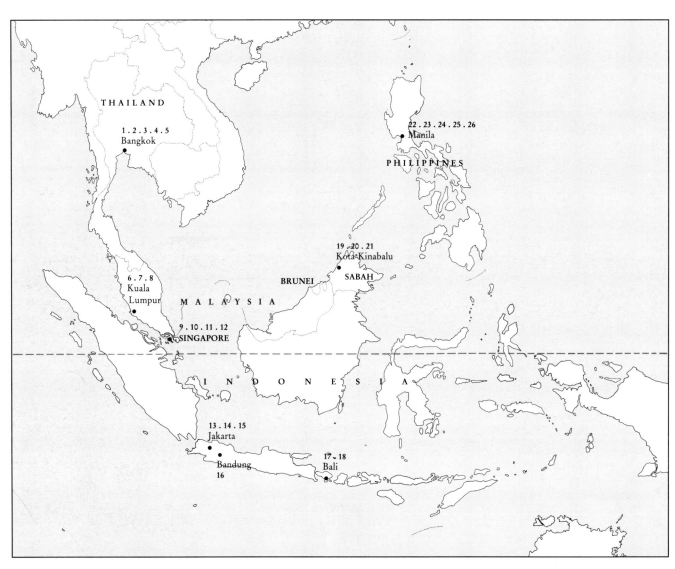

0 100   500km

1 The Tiptus House	9 The Reuter House	19 The Tengku Adlin House
2 Bann Ton Son	10 The Wong House	20 The Razak Harris House
3 Bann Rim Nam	11 The Mountbatten House	21 The Lo House
4 Bann Soi Klang	12 The Bing Tong Park House	22 The Locsin House
5 The Vacharphol House	13 The Gunawan House	23 The Mañosa House
6 The Eu House	14 The Moersid House	24 The Zulueta House
7 The Precima House	15 The Indra Abidin House	25 The Roa House
8 The Roof Roof House	16 The Sunaryo House	26 The Tesoro Rest House
	17 The Hadiprana House	
	18 The Giusti House	